Classics of Fashion

Classics of Fashion

Harriet Worsley

ISBN 1-84044-100-3

Produced by:
The Brown Reference Group plc
8 Chapel Place
Rivington Street
London EC2A 3DQ, UK
www.brownpartworks.co.uk

Editor: Sarah Halliwell
Designer: Helen James
Picture Researcher: Susannah Jayes
Managing Editor: Tim Cooke
Editorial Director: Lindsey Lowe
Art Director: Dave Goodman
Production Director: Alastair Gourlay

This book is dedicated to Jamie Knight.

The author would like to thank Virginia Worsley, Daniel Worsley, and Shami Senthi for
their assistance.

Picture Credits

AFP: 50. Advertising Archives: 22, 40, 51, 70, 98, 104, 134, 162, 174. Associated Press: 60. Brown Reference
Group: 26, 99, 102, 110. Camera Press: 13, 31, 32, 44, 113. Corbis: 146, 158; Bettmann 45; BVD 124; Tim Graham 86;
Corin Krasner 112; Steve Rayner 27; Trinette Reed 8; Jacqueline Sallow 36; Sygma 140, 169. European Press
Photo Agency: 14. Getty Images News Services: 126. Hulton Archive: 10, 12, 20, 30, 68, 74, 82, 90, 108, 128, 132,
136, 148, 151, 152, 160, 164. Kobal Collection: Spelling/ABC 120. Dr Martens:118. Alexander McQueen: 114. ©
Duane Michals/courtesy Pace/MacGill Gallery, New York. Popperfoto: 28, 72, 130, 154. Press Association: 88.
Retna: 76. Rex Features: 16, 24, 34, 38, 42, 49, 54, 58, 52, 78, 94, 96, 100, 111, 116, 122, 125, 142, 144, 156, 166, 170,
172. Robert Hunt Library : 64, 92. Roger-Viollet:168. Schott: 106. Topham: 18, 46, 48, 56, 80, 138. Victoria &
Albert Museum Picture Library: 52, 66, 150.
Front Cover: Rex Features. Back Cover: Hulton Archive

Printed and bound in Hong Kong

1 2 3 4 5   06 05 04 03 02

CONTENTS

INTRODUCTION

It was 1901, and the bubble finally burst. The Victorian era came to an end with the death of its namesake, who had worn mourning black for 40 years. Society waved goodbye to sobriety and restraint, and never looked back. The party was about to begin. The daring threw off their bustles and corsets. Waistlines shunted up to the bust. Thanks to designers such as Paul Poiret, women began to enjoy freedom and movement. The fashionable embraced bright color and opulence, and fluttered about streets and race meetings like exotic butterflies.

With the Roaring Twenties came a cult for youth, and androgynous girls with scandalously short skirts and cropped hair. Out went womanly curves and in came the straight up-and-down look with its dropped waists and gym-slip dresses. Economics and cloth shortages dictated that World War II fashion was figure-hugging and mean. By the 1950s women were hungry for voluptuous Dior-style dresses with wide skirts. Youth began to assert itself sartorially. The new generation had money to spend on clothes and records. The height of teenage cool was a gingham dress after Brigitte Bardot or a bad-boy black leather jacket after Marlon Brando.

By the Swinging Sixties, the curvaceous look was out of fashion again. Grown women wanted to look like little girls—naturally, some failed. Little Lolitas dreamt of Mary Quant's mini-pinafore dresses, Vidal Sassoon crops, and high life on the King's Road. Youth took over. It ran the shops, rioted in the streets, made the music, set the trends. Coco Chanel famously complained: "I like fashion to go down into the street, but I can't accept that it should originate there." But street style and youth culture were to have a major influence for the rest of the century. Ideas from the street influenced high fashion, while catwalk trends were reinterpreted for the mainstream.

Flower power took off. The hippies went to Woodstock while the middle classes played safe with Laura Ashley florals. Clever Vivienne Westwood set a street fashion trend with the punk movement, but went on to make her name as a high fashion designer. The 1980s had its glittering Dynasty power dressing. Sportswear came out of the locker-room, into the street, and onto the catwalk. By the 1990s trends were shifting so fast that new looks emerged every six months. Grunge, the minimal look, the retro hippie look and even the retro punk look all came and went. There was always something for everyone.

We owe how we dress today to a handful of designers who dared to step out of line, challenge the status quo, and break taboos: Christian Dior with his daringly wide skirts; Issey Miyake with his futuristic approach; Miuccia

Prada with her pared down synthetic handbags; and the mistress of all innovation—Coco Chanel, who broke all the rules with unrivalled style. Christian Dior once observed: "No one person can change fashion—a big fashion change imposes itself." But the skill is in picking up on that new mood or feeling of change.

It would be a mistake to evaluate a century of fashion just by its clothing designers. As important were the accessories designers, the craftsmen and women who could make unparalleled luxury goods: Manolo Blahnik with his shoes, Louis Vuitton and his luggage.... Nor should we forget the entrepreneurs, who create brand names and use clever retailing and marketing to make their products sell and sell and sell: Calvin Klein with his underwear, Levi Strauss and his jeans, Ralph Lauren and his cowboy look. These entrepreneurs treated fashion as a business. And they reaped the benefits.

Fashion cannot exist without someone to buy and wear the clothes. Throughout the century high-profile men and women have helped to make a trend just by being seen, filmed, or photographed. In the 1930s Hollywood held sway over fashion. High-street stores gave over whole departments to glamour, and designers stood in line to dress the stars—but it was a politician's wife, Jackie Kennedy, who was the biggest style icon of the lot. From the 1960s pop-stars began to endorse trends and teenage fans quickly copied. The Beatles, Madonna, Boy George, The Sex Pistols, and even Kurt Cobain lived fast, sometimes died young, and made their mark on the fashion hall of fame. By the 1990s it was the supermodels, Naomi Campbell, Christy Turlington, Linda Evangelista, and then Kate Moss, who led fashion. The tables had turned. The models once only considered as glorified coat-hangers became stars in their own right.

The 84 entries in *Classics of Fashion* are by no means a complete guide to who's who in 20th-century fashion. Other names and subjects could fill many more pages. But the book is a snapshot of some of the great and the good of a hundred years of fashion. The subjects have been chosen not only for their aesthetic value, but for being innovative, commercial successes, withstanding the test of time, or capturing the spirit of an era. Each entry is a classic in the sense that it made its mark, changed the course of fashion history, and influenced the way we dress today, from the little black dress to Johnny Rotten's God Save the Queen T-shirt and Alexander McQueen's Highland Rape collection. Queen Victoria would not be amused.

THE AFRO

fashion classic • 1968

"Say it loud—I'm black and I'm proud, Now we demand a chance to do things for ourself, We're tired of beatin' our head against the wall, And workin' for someone else." So sang James Brown in 1968. In the late 1960s, the Black Power movement kicked out at white America and the Afro haircut became a political statement. You couldn't miss it. The hair stood on end in a large sphere, as if an electric current had shot through its owner. The new style rejected the straightening and lightening techniques traditionally used on black hair to make it conform to white ideals of beauty. The Afro became a proud symbol for the celebration of blackness and the fight for the black cause.

Ninety sixty-eight was the year of the Afro for black American men and women. They used their hair as a form of expression, just as their white hippie counterparts were using long hair to signal youth and independence. Militant Angela Davis, famed for being on the FBI's ten most wanted list, took up the Afro style. Singer Sly Stone toured Britain and the U.S. with an Afro cut. And Marsha Hunt, star of hippie musical *Hair* and mother of Mick Jagger's child, flaunted hers at the Isle of Wight pop festival in England in 1969.

The Afro was a sign of the times, a sign of change, and a sign of the fight for black independence. Wearing an Afro in the late 1960s said: "I'm black and I'm proud."

Ninety sixty-eight was also the year that the Black Panthers, foremost among black activists, made their mark. They combined their Afros—when they weren't in jail—with dashing black leather and Cuban heels. Some Black Panthers wore their Afros wild and natural. But once the look became fashionable, a perfect Afro sphere needed combing, spraying, and visits to the hairdresser to keep it in shape. And those who couldn't cope with going the whole way could fake it. Diana Ross sang her heart out at the Royal Variety Show in London in 1968 wearing a bold Afro wig.

The Afro was a sign of the times, a sign of change, and a sign of the fight for black independence. James Brown sang about Black Power, but those with Afros didn't even have to open their mouths. Wearing an Afro in the late 1960s in itself said: "I'm black and I'm proud."

The striking Afro haircut has always made a strong statement. In the 1960s it was about politics—today, it's more about fashion.

QUEEN ALEXANDRA

fashion icon • 1844–1925

With Queen Victoria finally dead and buried, the new King Edward VII and his Danish bride, Alexandra, gave society the chance to let loose. They partied, traveled, and presided over the social scene. The Edwardian era lasted only from 1901 to 1910, but it set the tone for the century.

Despite being 58 years old when crowned Queen, the tall, slim, elegant Alexandra was a style leader. Her regal posture and long neck were ideal for showing off clothes and jewelry. The Alexandra signature style was a poodle-fringe hairdo, tailored suits for travel, and a heavily made-up face. The most accessible and copied trends endorsed by the Queen were high-collared dresses and blouses and jeweled choker necklaces, or "dog collars." The most extreme of these multistrand chokers started just above the cleavage and stretched right up to under the chin, pulling tight over the throat. Alexandra also popularized neckbands of velvet pinned with a brooch. Rumor had it that she wore them to hide a small disfiguring scar on her neck, but society copied her regardless.

Vita Sackville-West chronicled the look in her novel *The Edwardians*. (Button, the maid, dresses the Duchess, while the Duchess talks to her son and heir, Sebastian): "Button, gathering up the lovely mass of taffeta and tulle, held the bodice open while the Duchess flung off her wrap and dived gingerly into the billows of her dress.... Then she encircled her throat with the dog-collar of rubies and diamonds, tied with a large bow of white tulle at the back. 'You must choose a wife who will do credit to the jewels, Sebastian,' she said as she slipped an earring into place."

The royal couple favored amethysts, peridots, and pearls, while fashionable ladies preferred platinum or white gold, and diamonds set with pearls.

The elegant Queen was a highly influential figure. That the fashionable copied her chokers may have been some consolation to Alexandra at a time when her husband's mistresses—Lillie Langtry and Alice Keppel among them—were the obsession of the public. But society sometimes took its emulation of Alexandra to extremes. When she hurt her knee after rheumatic fever, rumor had it that some women even copied her resulting awkward walk, naming it the Alexandra Glide. They should have stuck with the dog collars.

Queen Alexandra (1844–1925), wife of King Edward VII. Fashionable
society copied her style, from her choker necklaces to her hairdo.

ANORAK

fashion classic • 1920s

Those who think that "anorak" is just a nickname for nerds, trainspotters, and old men in nylon clothes may be surprised to learn that anoraks also have something to do with fashion. The word "anorak" comes from Alaska's Aleutian Islands; the word "parka" (a longer anorak) is the name for coats in Greenland. The Greenland Inuits snuggled up in their hip-length hooded jackets of sealskin to keep out the cold.

During the 1920s, *Vogue* pictured a female aviator in a thigh-length, mink-trimmed hooded suede anorak. In World War II, Britain's Royal Air Force introduced anoraks, or windcheaters, for pilots. These incorporated a flying hat and jacket all in one. After the war, civilians took up the style for skiing—elongated waist-hugging parkas and blouson-shaped anoraks. They came in bright colors, prints, and quilting, in waterproofed wool or nylon. Hoods could be zipped on and off, or rolled into a zippered collar.

With the 1960s came a craze for experimental synthetics—big plastic zippers and silk-nylon fabric mixes. Spot, stripe, and daisy prints came in bright colors, and silver looked the most modern. Off the slopes, the parka (now a longer, looser, hooded version) came back into fashion with the Mods, the British youth group who wore U.S. army surplus M-51 field parkas. Their coats protected their suits when they kicked up the dust on their Vespas.

The Mods influenced the oversized long anoraks adopted during the 1980s, from hip-hop boys to preppies. *Elle* wrote in 1990: "Discover the new parka. Active, practical, stylish—this year's crucial statement is lightweight and hooded, brilliantly coloured, loosely tailored…." The anorak was no longer just a practical garment. *Vogue* shot a model wearing nothing but a transparent blue blouson anorak and a satin hotpants. Anoraks were designed for the evening in fabrics such as silk.

So when you see those men in anoraks standing at the end of Platform 19 with their notebooks, remember their fashionable counterparts.

"His and hers" quilted anoraks from 1967. Waterproof, lightweight, and fur-lined, these coats were perfect for stylish skiing.

GIORGIO ARMANI

men's suit • 1974

Giorgio Armani's suit liberated men from sharp, constricting tailoring and allowed them to relax and move. Armani launched his menswear line in 1974 with his revolutionary suit design. His idea was to add volume, relax the silhouette, and simplify the construction. He whipped out linings, interfaces, and trouser creases. He moved buttons and pads. He adjusted the slope of the shoulders, cut the lapels narrow, and added baggy pockets. An Armani suit didn't rely on perfect fit, so he cut generously and used fluid, loose-weave linens and wools. His muted colors and woven stripes and checks looked almost feminine.

The key to his success was creating comfortable, flattering suits that were more like sportswear than traditional formal clothes. They were still smart and businesslike, but gave the impression of perfect ease. It was a winning formula. Famously, Richard Gere wore an Armani suit in his 1980 film *American Gigolo*. "Armani may have invented the unconstructed suit, but he didn't own it for long. In fashion, imitation has always been the fastest path to popularity, and Armani knockoffs popped up faster than dandelions in a backyard," wrote Teri Agins in *The End of Fashion*.

> *The key to Giorgio Armani's success was creating comfortable, flattering suits that were more like sportswear than traditional formal clothes.*

Armani then turned to women's tailoring, and gave it the same treatment. The result was to create an almost androgynous working dress for men and women. Where his man's suit now looked more understated and feminine, his woman's suit seemed stronger, more masculine and powerful than its predecessors. Naturally this appealed to the decade's power-hungry female executives, and by the end of the 1970s, Armani had widened and padded the shoulders for the infamous power uniform of the 1980s.

In 1981 Armani launched a secondary, cheaper line, Emporio Armani, so that rather than going elsewhere to get its Armani copies, the public could come to straight to him for the real thing. It was a smooth move. Men's formal dressing would never be the same again.

When Giorgio Armani's suits first hit the catwalk, they were revolutionary—a winning combination of smartness and comfort.

LAURA ASHLEY

floral frock • 1970s

Imagine dreamy, soft focus cottages, meadows of flowers, a waft of wild roses, country damsels in floral cotton dresses picnicking by clear streams.... This was the nostalgic country idyll that Laura Ashley conjured up in the 1970s. When a woman slipped into a Laura Ashley dress, she felt transported back in time to a world free from mass-production and modernity. This was something new—a direct contrast to the space-age mania of the 1960s. The Laura Ashley phenomenon symbolized back to nature and family values. Middle-class women couldn't get enough of it. This was a clean-living version of flower power that couldn't be farther away from marching for your rights, LSD, and Janis Joplin.

As luck would have it, hemlines came tumbling down at the end of the 1960s and the maxiskirt came back into fashion. It couldn't have been better for Laura Ashley, with her trademark florals and natural fabrics. Suddenly a generation of women were dressing like milkmaids in her flowing, comfortable, floral sprigged dresses. She decorated full-length, high-collared neo-Victorian and Edwardian dresses with flounces, puffed sleeves, and yards of broderie anglaise. She layered cotton or corduroy pinafores over crisp white underdresses, reminiscent of Victorian nightshirts and petticoats.

Suddenly a generation of women were dressing like milkmaids in Laura Ashley's flowing, comfortable, floral-sprigged dresses.

It was a handicraft exhibition at London's Victoria & Albert Museum that first inspired Laura Ashley to design fabric based on original eighteenth- and nineteenth-century prints. With her ex-stockbroker husband, Bernard Ashley, she set up a cottage industry designing headscarves and dishtowels from their kitchen in Wales. Then they tried clothes—aprons, ovengloves, and gardening smocks—and sold the first Laura Ashley dress for $9 in 1968. In the early days they outsourced work to Welsh housewives, who would literally sit by the fireside and stitch collars and cuffs.

This was just the humble beginning for Laura Ashley, the entrepreneur who offered women romance and escapism. Her business was to mushroom into an empire.

Laura Ashley built her successful fashion and homeware empire on pretty, timeless flower-print dresses.

LÉON BAKST

Ballets Russes costumes • 1909

Léon Bakst influenced a generation with his vibrant costume and set designs for the Ballets Russes. Paris had never seen anything like it. A Ballets Russes performance was a visual and musical feast, overseen by producer Sergei Diaghilev. He brought together some of the greatest creative geniuses of the time—composers Prokofiev and Ravel; dancers Nijinsky and Pavlova; artists Picasso and Matisse; and designer Léon Bakst.

The Russian ballet company came to Paris in 1909 and performed *Cleopatra*. Bakst designed the opulent costumes—he swathed bodies in gold and hung hair with strings of pearls. With 1910 came *Scheherazade*, the ballet that made Bakst's name. Its subject matter was scandalous—ladies of the harem indulging in their fantasies with a troop of black slaves against a voluptuous backdrop of drapes, cushions, and carpets. The dancers wore pantaloons, loose paisley dresses, turbans on their heads, and feathers in their hair. The costumes revealed tantalizing segments of naked flesh. And for the production of *L'Après-midi d'un Faune*, Nijinsky danced in a skintight leotard, a bunch of grapes at his genitals. Critics labeled the Ballets Russes "degenerate" and called Bakst "an erotomanic."

> *Ladies exchanged muted colors and rustling taffeta for loose dresses and the rich hues of Bakst's designs.*

Bakst's vibrant costume designs had a major influence on fashion. The dancers—twirling, twisting, and exalting in the freedom of their loose clothes—contrasted with the audience sitting stiffly in their formal dresses, corsets, and collars. Taking their cue from Bakst, and the Oriental fever washing over Paris, designers such as Paul Poiret and Jeanne Paquin began dressing the fashionable set in voluminous harem pants, turbanned or ostrich-plumed headdresses, and lavish kimono dresses. Ladies exchanged muted colors and rustling taffeta for loose dresses and the rich hues of Bakst's designs.

Bakst inspired a generation with his insight into the fairytale magic of ancient Egypt and secret harems, at a time when only the privileged few would ever experience the Orient for real. The world was entranced.

Vera Fokina and Mikhail Fokine of the Ballets Russes wearing Bakst costumes from Scheherazade, *in about 1910.*

CRISTOBAL BALENCIAGA

sack dress • 1956

The Picasso of fashion. The master of couture. The Paris-based, Spanish-born couturier Cristobal Balenciaga is still a design legend, lauded for his intellectual, sculptural cutting techniques and sense of color.

The dominating silhouette of the 1950s was Christian Dior's New Look—nipped-in waist and ballooning ballerina skirts. But Balenciaga strove to remove the waist completely. His 1947 sack, or barrel, line jackets hung away from the skin, drawing into the body only at the hem, and his 1955 tunic line erased the waist altogether.

But the greatest achievement was his chemise dress of 1956. It hung loosely over the torso and hips, and then tapered down to fit snugly over the knees, stopping just below. As with the straight-up-and-down flapper dresses of Balenciaga's childhood, it was as if the waist didn't exist. Disparaging journalists nicknamed it the sack dress. The *Herald Tribune* couldn't come to terms with it: "The ungainly chemise is everywhere, yet boys date the girls as eagerly as ever."

The term "sack" had been used before. When the creative Austrian collective the Wiener Werkstätte launched its reform dresses in 1911, similar to the caftan dresses worn in Gustav Klimt's paintings, they were criticized for looking like flour sacks.

Though deemed unwomanly and unflattering, Balenciaga's sack dress was copied and copied by manufacturers cashing in on the trend. Designers Hubert de Givenchy and Dior did their own waistless dresses, Givenchy exaggerating the look to extreme proportions. The *Vogue Pattern Book* grudgingly included it in 1957: "The loose 'sack line' and resultant loss of the waist was a recent Paris drama, but in retrospect we find a more balanced picture. The semi-fitting silhouette, bypassing the waist and touching the hips, is an important trend."

Balenciaga's sack dress bridged the 1950s and the 1960s, anticipating the 1960s square-cut and trapeze lines that banished the natural body shape from sight. The success of Balenciaga's sack dress pioneered the look of the following decade, and helped change the perception that only the womanly silhouette was acceptable.

A bonbon pink satin cape by Balenciaga from 1965, a decade after the original "sack" dress. His loose line was endlessly copied.

BARBOUR COAT

fashion classic • 1894

The sight of a waxed green Barbour coat, the British uniform of fishermen, Sloane Rangers (preppies), and farmers, conjures up wet walks in bracken and Land Rovers. But its heritage stretches back over a hundred years.

Scottish farmer John Barbour took the rain and gales head on while tending his sheep. But he soon came down from the hills, exchanging farming for a warmer, drier life in town. He set up J. Barbour and Sons in 1894. The company made protective oilskins for North Sea fishermen, rivermen, dockers, and sailors. Mr. Barbour used the beacon that welcomed the seamen into South Shields harbor as his company motif. The word spread, and soon land-loving farmers, carters, laborers, and shepherds wanted his oilskins too. "The driest spot on Earth is the inside of a Beacon Coat," proclaimed the 1913 Barbour catalog.

In World War II, Captain George Philips asked for the Barbour all in one oversuit to be chopped in two, to make separate jackets and trousers for his submarine crew. He was also a motorbike enthusiast, and Barbour jackets and matching trousers became the favorite gear for British motorbike racing. Army motorcycle display teams wore them, as did patrolmen from 14 different police forces. A 1954 catalog entry boasted: "Built to stand the hard conditions of competition riding, it is Britain's toughest suit. It … is the accepted outfit for motor-cycling wear. You know you are properly clad in the Barbour international suit."

Today's jacket is made from Egyptian cotton. The thread and finished fabric are both waterproofed, and the double-thickness seams ensure that no water can sneak in. The finishing touches are brass studs, large-tooth metal zippers, and adjustable storm cuffs that can be tightened to keep out the rain. Large flap-top pockets have rounded corners to avoid snagging on brambles and barbed wire, and side pockets are lined in moleskin to keep the hands warm.

In the early 1990s, the Barbour became a street uniform for poseur urban Italians, but the Barbour jacket always looks its best worn in the country and battered by the elements. And it is exactly what John Barbour would have dreamed of in the lashing rain on the Scottish hills more than a century ago.

Modern Barbour advertising promotes the combination of hardiness
and style that has made the waterproof coat a fashion classic.

BRIGITTE BARDOT

fashion icon • born 1934

Brigitte Bardot flung gingham back into the fashion arena when she wore a candy-pink checked wedding dress for her marriage to co-star Jacques Charrier in 1959. Designer Jacques Esterel masterminded the scoop neck, neat nipped-in waist, three-quarter-length sleeves, and wide rock-'n'-roll skirt. The overall look was girlish and innocent, yet devastatingly sexy, emphasizing the curves of Bardot's pert figure. Esterel, previously a dealer in machine tools, had started work as a fashion designer in 1958. Bardot's commission helped to launch his career.

BB, as she was known, broke with wedding protocol and convention. She let her shaggy blonde mane hang loose. She chose simple checked cotton and linen rather than the traditional silk-organdie, brocade, and lace. Bardot put the sex back into American-pie country gingham—and her fans loved it. Once Europe and the United States got their hands on the wedding photographs, the dress was copied again and again. Women, and particularly teenagers, wanted that dress for everything that it stood for—love, informality, sexiness, girlishness, womanhood.

French former model Bardot looked younger than her peers of the silver screen, and quickly became a teen icon. She was one of the few non-Hollywood stars ever to make it big in the movies. Like Marilyn Monroe, Bardot rejected the fastidious, offscreen groomed image of many stars for a relaxed, resort-style chic popular with teenagers at the time. Her perfect sun-bronzed figure, messy blonde hair, and black rimmed eyes oozed sex appeal. She became indelibly linked with glamorous resort St. Tropez, where her 1956 film *And God Created Woman* was shot. Her character swung between a knowing sensuality and naivety, which men found irresistible and women wanted to copy. The movie earned her fame and a nickname: the Sex Kitten.

The late 1950s saw scores of Bardot wannabes riding pillion in pink gingham behind their leather-jacketed boyfriends. Some teamed it with a matching scarf pulled over their hair. Others wore gingham bikinis, gingham Capri pants, and wide rock-'n'-roll gingham skirts.

Brigitte Bardot wears gingham in Les Petroleuses *in 1971 and (above right) at her wedding in 1959.*

*Made popular in the 1920s and 1930s by sports fans, baseball caps
are now a ubiquitous accessory, worn by everyone from streetwise
kids to paparazzi-shy celebs.*

BASEBALL CAP

fashion classic • 1920s

Originally, baseball batters wore caps that sat neatly over the head like brimless skullcaps. Then the New York Yankees legend Babe Ruth helped to popularize a visored cap. The hardened crown protected the head from stray balls while the visor shaded the face from the sun. Fans took to wearing caps bearing their favorite team colors and emblems. Players like Babe Ruth and Joe Dimaggio (who married Marilyn Monroe) became the United States' heroes and role models, the Michael Jordans of the 1920s and 1930s.

The baseball cap successfully made the transition from the sports pitch to the street, becoming part of the casual uniform of truckers and workers. Then, in the 1960s and 1970s, Hispanic and African Americans took it up. It reached the pinnacle of cool on the heads of the hip-hop fraternity and B-boys in the 1980s and 1990s. Some wore their caps with visors facing to the side or the back of the head; others perched them high on top of the head. They teamed them with sweatsuits and sneakers.

But baseball caps were also practical—they served as head protection for break dancing headspins on the dancefloor (although most now had a soft crown). At their most sinister, they served as a uniform for street crime and gangsters. In Compton, where rival gangs the Crips and the Bloods wage war, you can be gunned down for wearing a red cap in a "blue" neighborhood. Nelson George reported in the *Village Voice* in 1989: "L.L. Cool J is rhyming for several thousand whites, blacks, and latinos. The stage comes complete with flashing lights, dancing girls, and guest rapper Busy Bee.... But the Crips in the house don't care where the show is supposed to be. In the arena's darkness a posse of ten to 15 of them, their blue colors no longer camouflaged under black caps, jackets, and jeans, reveal themselves. Not long afterward a scuffle ensues and a brother in a white Le Coq Sportif sweatsuit goes down."

Surfers, skate kids, roadies, and rock rebels wear baseball caps to look cool. It is the ultimate all-American unisex accessory worn by everyone. But when, in the 1990s, British politician William Hague tried to update his image by wearing one emblazoned with "HAGUE," he was ridiculed. When it comes to style, it isn't what you wear, it's the way that you wear it.

Looking dapper in their collarless jackets, Paul, George, Ringo, and John make some final sartorial adjustments before a live show.

THE BEATLES

the Nehru jacket • 1960s

They were the Fab Four—John Lennon, Paul McCartney, Ringo Starr, and George Harrison. The mop-topped Beatles changed popular culture for ever with their Merseyside version of rock 'n'roll and its poetic love songs and catchy harmonies. "You have to be a real sour square not to love the nutty, noisy, happy, handsome Beatles," claimed the *Daily Mirror* in 1963.

The Beatles had power. They could make or break fashion trends. Where the Beatles went, youth followed, and all the establishment could do was watch. *The New Statesman* wrote in 1964: "Conservative candidates have been officially advised to mention them whenever possible in their speeches. The Queen expressed concern about the length of Ringo's hair. Young diplomats at our Washington embassy fought for their autographs."

By 1962, The Beatles had dumped their leather jackets and T shirts for a new, grown-up style influenced by couturier Pierre Cardin. They wore skinny-legged trousers with square-cut, round-necked collarless jackets made for them by tailor Dougie Millings.

After a trip to India, Cardin introduced Nehru jackets into his collection. The slimline jacket with no lapels and a neat stand-up collar took its name from Indian prime minister, Jawaharlal Nehru, who often wore one. The staff in Cardin's boutique began to wear Nehru jackets to work. They looked their best worn over one of Cardin's turtlenecks.

The Beatles adopted them, flouting convention by leaving their ties behind and wearing Nehru jackets as an alternative to traditional suit jackets. The Nehru jacket helped to bridge the gap between Mod-influenced 1960s clothing and the hippies' flowing bohemian layers It looked sharp as a neat suit, but it evoked India, travel, and the hippie trail.

The Beatles were no strangers to India. In 1967, they left to study with the Maharishi Mahesh Yogi, grew their hair, studied the sitar with Ravi Shankar, and started to introduce the mystical magic of Indian music into their songs. And in The Beatles' film, *Yellow Submarine*, Ringo appeared as an animated cartoon character wearing bell-bottoms, Beatle boots, a Nehru jacket, and a beard. Inevitably, the world fell in behind.

BIKINI

fashion classic • 1946

Women loved it, the Catholic Church denounced it, and starlets have made history in it.

When Louis Réard revealed his scandalous bikini design on a curvaceous showgirl at a Paris swimming pool in 1946, the world sat up, gasped with shock, and took note. The ex-mechanical engineer had been designing two-piece swimwear since the 1920s. But he had chosen the right time to patent his little invention and to open a shop in Paris to pedal his designs.

The same year, furrier and womenswear designer Jacques Heim also launched his "atome" slinky two-piece as part of his beach collection. It was only when the 1954 American H bomb test at Bikini Atoll rocked the South Pacific that the atome was renamed the bikini, and it stuck.

The bikini was revolutionary. It dared women to reveal more flesh. Never before had they had the chance to show midriffs and navels in public. In postwar liberated France, times were hard, but sea air and sunbathing on the sand was a cheap day out. The bikini was a symbol of freedom and marked a return to simple pleasures now the Nazis had left. The risqué fashion swept along the coastlines. By the 1950s, the itsy bitsy teeny two-piece covered with artificial flowers was festooning the assets of France's best. Not so in the United States—the bikini was deemed indecent, and was only widely accepted there in the mid-1960s.

The bikini has since been the ultimate attention-seeking garment for nubile starlets in search of the limelight. Once it hit the mainstream, women used it to their advantage. And some were unforgettable. Diana Dors wore a mink one at Cannes. A few strips of animal hide gave Raquel Welch a shred of decency in *One Million Years B.C.* (1966). Nubile Brigitte Bardot made a splash in frilled gingham in *And God Created Woman* (1956), and Bond girl Ursula Andress stalked seductively out of the sea in a white bikini in *Dr. No* (1962). If you've got it, why not flaunt it?

A two-piece toweling swimsuit from the late 1940s. The daring style
of beachwear did not become known as a bikini until 1954.

31

So prestigious is the Manolo Blahnik label that some obsessive fans

buy his shoes to display in glass cases rather than to wear.

MANOLO BLAHNIK

stiletto • 1980s

As a child, Manolo Blahnik made miniature shoes for lizards, dogs, and cats at his home on the Canary Islands. Today, the feet of the richest women in the world slide into his high heels. Manolo stilettos are the Rolls Royces of the shoe world. Exquisitely handmade, and with a price tag of several hundred dollars, they are the shoes of dreams.

When, in 1970, Blahnik showed his theater designs to Diana Vreeland, editor-in-chief of American *Vogue*, she spotted a genius and backed him all the way, encouraging him to focus on shoes. He had no formal training, but he did have a love of footwear. He opened his first shop, Zapata, in 1973. And he never looked back.

Manolo stilettos are known for their brightly colored leather, tapered toe, and high, high heels. When a woman puts on a pair of Manolo spikes, she gets comfort (well, as comfortable as high heels will allow) and sexiness in one delicate package. The shoes are almost weightless with their minute straps, delicate soles, and slivers of heels. Yet, almost impossibly, the heels are strong enough to support a human body.

Salvatore Ferragamo is credited with inventing the reinforcing steel bar that makes stilettos possible, but it was Blahnik who took the trashiness out of stilettos and made them chic. He can transform women into goddesses on pedestals. His elongating spikes made the 1980s working woman feel she was really something, particularly when she wore them with a power suit.

Manolo stilettos are almost weightless, with their minute straps, delicate soles, and slivers of heels. Yet the heels are strong enough to support a human body.

Blahnik's heels may be excessive and his designs theatrical, but the shoes are amazingly beautiful and never vulgar. Blahnik weaves a fantasy about the fictional women who inspire each shoe, from African princesses to street-smart Italian girls. His imagination reels with electric pink slingbacks and bright yellow mules shimmying with red-petal tassels. He is a man obsessed with his craft.

DAVID BOWIE

fashion icon • born 1947

David Bowie welcomed his fans to London's Royal Festival Hall in 1972 with the words: "Hello, I'm Ziggy Stardust." The same year, the boy from Bromley released an album called *The Rise And Fall of Ziggy Stardust and the Spiders from Mars*, and then spent the next two years living up to it. Ziggy Stardust became his alter ego and theatrical sci-fi stage persona. He wowed his fans with flamboyant performances, slipping his feline body in and out of progressively wilder outfits for each show. Designer Kansai Yamamoto put him in costumes inspired by Japanese kabuki theater. He dyed his hair bright red and spiked it with lacquer. He wore makeup and dressed in bright jumpsuits, glitter outfits, and platform shoes. He stood out like a shiny futuristic alien against the drab backdrop of leftover flower children and Laura Ashley smocks.

Bowie groupies loved his glam rock look, and both sexes copied it. A 1973 article in *Music Scene* reported: "For all his 'fag' image, nowhere is he loved more than in traditionally 'earthy' working-class cities like Glasgow, Liverpool, Leeds ... All across the country on his last tour, boys, and girls, men and women were turning up in their Bowie makeup and garb. The zigzag from the *Aladdin Sane* sleeve ... [was] to be seen flashing from all parts of the auditorium."

Bowie encouraged both sexes to dress up in glitter and glam. Boys no longer had to be the dowdy counterpart. He broke the taboos between male and female dress.

David Bowie ushered in a new asexual androgyny. The hippies had gone for unisex by dressing down in jeans, T-shirts, and matching long hair. But Bowie encouraged both sexes to dress up in glitter and glam. Boys no longer had to be the dowdy counterpart. He broke the taboos between male and female traditional dress with a flourish of his feather boa. His final punch at the traditionalists was the claim, in a 1972 *Melody Maker* interview, that he was bisexual.

Other glam rockers followed in his wake—Marc Bolan, Gary Glitter, Alvin Stardust. *Music Scene* wrote: "What ... is it all coming to? When even the men, the 'real' men with broad masculine physiques are camping it up. 'It's all coming out into the open,' grins David, 'and I love it.'"

David Bowie on stage in London in July 1973. His androgynous look and theatrical dressing made him a unique fashion icon.

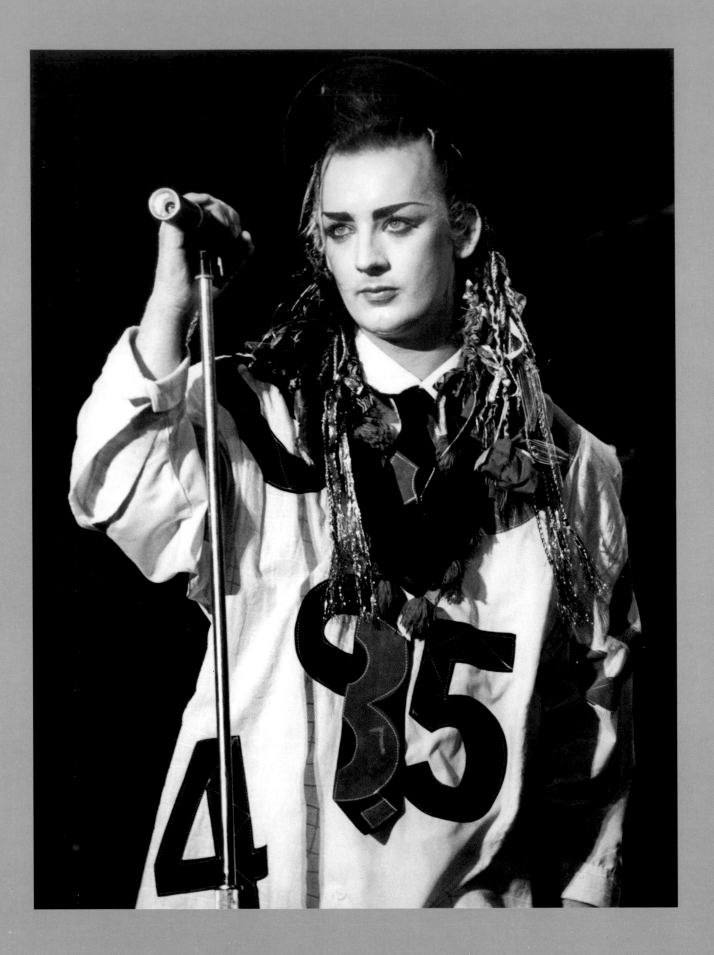

BOY GEORGE

fashion icon • born 1961

Number one "gender bender" and popstar Boy George was not prepared to blend into the background. You couldn't miss him with his rabbi hat, dreadlocks, painted face, and loud smocks worn over trousers. His Irish father wanted him to join the family building firm, but when schoolboy George O'Dowd dyed his hair bright orange as a tribute to his hero David Bowie, the seeds of rebellion were already sown. And, just like David Bowie, Boy George's look was not transvestite, but rather a man stealing from the female preserve of dressing up. Why should men be shy about flaunting their feathers?

British singers Boy George and Adam Ant were part of the New Romantic movement, an off-shoot of punk that attracted fashion-conscious posers who quickly tired of punk's hardening violent edge. Visionary designer Vivienne Westwood fueled the look with her swashbuckling 1981 Pirate collection, complete with breeches and ruffled shirts. The New Romantics congregated in frills and frippery in London's clubland.

Boy George was a regular at the legendary Blitz club, and soon became renowned on the New Romantic club circuit for his outrageous and theatrical costumes. He managed to offend both the Rastafarian and Jewish communities with his bizarre signature style. And when he smashed into the big time as lead singer of Culture Club in the early 1980s, with songs such as "Karma Chameleon," his television appearances took the androgynous look out of the underground and slammed it into the sitting rooms of middle England. What must they have thought?

> *Boy George's look was not transvestite, but rather a man stealing from the female preserve of dressing up. Why should men by shy about flaunting their feathers?*

"I'm a poof with muscles, but underneath all these clothes and makeup I am a very ordinary person," he reputedly said. He was also an icon. At the height of Boy George's career, fans bought as many posters of him as they did records, and both male and female groupies dressed like him. Boy George was an original, a one-off, and the man who brought gender-bender New Romantic style to the masses.

Boy George performing with Culture Club in the early 1980s. His painted face and dreadlocks inspired thousands of New Romantics.

MARLON BRANDO

fashion icon • born 1924

It's 1951. The silver screen. Marlon Brando stars as Stanley Kowalski in Tennessee Williams's *A Streetcar Named Desire*. The raw, brutish Stanley drinks, smokes, and shouts. He sexually satisfies his wife—and sexually assaults his sister-in-law (although the scene was censored). He wears a ripped, sweat-soaked white T-shirt, revealing every sinew and muscle of his torso. Slithers of his naked chest show through the torn fabric. Stanley is an animal (albeit a very good-looking one). The critics raged. And the film was a box-office hit.

Until now, a man would never, ever have worn a T-shirt in public. It was strictly underwear. Yet here was Brando as Stanley stalking around his apartment in his smalls, not bothering to cover up when his sister-in-law came to call.

During the heat of World War II, American soldiers had taken to wearing just T-shirts to keep cool. But undervests still weren't regarded as decent for normal civilian life. However, Brando's performance in *A Streetcar Named Desire* made such an impact that it changed attitudes to the T-shirt forever.

When he starred in the 1954 film *The Wild One*, Brando wore a white T-shirt with jeans and a leather jacket. Britain banned the film for over 10 years, apparently worried that teenagers would copy its lawless gangs and mood of rebellion. When Brando's character is asked, "What're you rebelling against, Johnnie?," he fires back, "What've ya got?" Inspired, 1950s youth aimed to look like biker boys by taking up his irresistible clothing combination.

Thanks mainly to Marlon Brando and his smoldering good looks, a white T-shirt became something sexually charged, manly, rough.

Thanks mainly to Marlon Brando and his smoldering good looks, a white T-shirt became something sexually charged, manly, rough. During the 1950s, to wear a white T-shirt without an overshirt became a sign of rebellious youth. And you could strut the streets in a white T-shirt without feeling half-dressed.

Marlon Brando glowers in a T-shirt in the hit movie A Streetcar Named Desire, *1951.*

Burberrys

OF LONDON

BURBERRY

Burberry mac • 1902

Burberry built its reputation on gabardine, the rain-resistant fabric made from waterproofed yarn. Thomas Burberry, a country sports outfitter, patented the fabric in 1902, and the beige Burberry mac became the favored country wet-weather gear of the upper classes. With King Edward VII in the habit of saying, "Give me my Burberry," the name stuck, and the company's waterproof coats simply became known as Burberrys.

To put the waterproofing to the test, Captain Robert F. Scott took a Burberry gabardine tent on his Antarctic expedition. Sir Ernest Shackelton was clothed by Burberry for his 1914 Antarctic exploration, which no doubt helped him survive his extraordinary hardships.

In World War I, British officers wore their belted knee-length Burberry coats in the trenches. Burberry adapted its mackintosh for the soldiers, adding epaulettes and D-rings for attaching equipment. A Burberry advertisement read: "The severest test that a Weatherproof can undergo is a campaign, involving exposure to every kind of weather for months on end, and it is under such conditions that the Tierlocken Burberry proves itself 'the most effectual safeguard ever invented.'" The belted macs became known as trenchcoats. After the war, rather than abandoning the practical trenchcoats, officers kept them for civilian life. The waterproof coat, with its distinctive checked lining, button-down storm flaps on one shoulder, and storm cuffs, was useful for staving off unexpected British showers. Greta Garbo helped to popularize the look when she wore one with her infamous slouch hat.

The Burberry trenchcoat enjoyed a fleeting revival in the late 1990s, when the chic and stylish wore them as a fashion item rather than a wet-weather basic. For a couple of seasons, the Burberry check became the hottest status symbol on the streets. Stylish advertisements starring high-profile models such as Kate Moss and Stella Tennant helped raise the label's profile. Burberry even launched a version of the trenchcoat for dogs—fashion victims could now keep their pooches safe and dry in Burberry gabardine.

The Burberry mac has remained a utilitarian classic, commonly worn as a top coat to protect a suit from the rain, and increasingly worn for city rather than country life.

The distinctive check of Thomas Burberry. His macs began as purely practical clothing, but became sought-after fashion items.

NAOMI CAMPBELL

fashion icon • born 1970

Billion-dollar babe and diva Naomi Campbell reached the peak of her modeling career in the late 1980s and early 1990s when she joined the ranks of what became known as the "super-models." It all started when photographer Steven Meisel shot Campbell, Christy Turlington, and Linda Evangelista in their underwear. They were nicknamed "the trinity," and suddenly every-one else wanted to photograph them too. These girls assumed the star status previously attrib-uted to actresses and singers, and demanded huge fees for appearances. As a result, the media put Campbell's personal life under the microscope, documenting her relationships with boxer Mike Tyson and actor Robert de Niro. She made catwalk history when she tumbled off a pair of Vivienne Westwood shoes over 10 inches (25cm) high, mercifully without snapping her ankles.

Elite model agent Beth Boldt had spotted the 15-year-old Campbell window-shopping in London's Covent Garden and asked her if she wanted to be a model. Naomi was already at theater and dance school, so performing in front of the camera came naturally.

As one of the most successful models of the century, Naomi challenged the typical blonde-haired, blue-eyed notion of beauty. She was French *Vogue*'s first black cover model. Designer Azzedine Alaïa nicknamed her the "Queen of the Catwalk." Her face has adorned the covers of many of the world's top fashion magazines. Naomi's near-perfect body, powerful catwalk strut, and ambitious nature helped her to fight her way to the top. Her chameleon beauty (she has Jamaican and Chinese ancestry) was perfect for the fashion designers in the late 1980s who needed a strong character to show off their power suits and logo-laden clothes.

Campbell gained a reputation for belonging to the tantrums and tiaras school of fashion, and certainly rubbed some people up the wrong way. Rachel Cooke wrote in the *Observer* in 2002: "Naomi Campbell is living proof that, contrary to popular belief, a woman CAN be too thin or too rich. In 1996, I had the misfortune to spend a day with the supermodel. She was so unpleas-ant that I've thanked my lucky stars for my enormous backside and diminutive bank balance ever since." Elite model agency refused to deal with her, her singing debut failed to make an impact, and she admitted drug addiction when she took the *Mirror* to court in 2002. But despite all that, Naomi Campbell remains one of the great beauties of the twentieth century.

Naomi Campbell remains as famous for allegations of divalike
behavior as for her supermodel looks.

CAPRI PANTS

fashion classic • 1950s

When Italian girls started leaping onto Vespas or Lambrettas and buzzing off, hell for leather, down narrow cobbled streets, they needed clothing that they knew wouldn't fly up or get caught. The solution was cropped mid-calf trousers, known as Capri pants, pirate pants, or pedal pushers. They wore them with flat shoes and windbreaking turtleneck sweaters. It was the 1950s and the scooter girls were the epitome of chic, modern, independent youth.

Italy was hip. The United States' stars flocked to Rome to make movies, to "Hollywood on the Tiber," as it was known. And Italy began to make its mark on the international fashion scene with a group of designers known for their luxury resort clothing. One was the aristocratic Emilio Pucci, "Emilio of

Capri," the designer who invented Capri pants. Pucci summered each year on the fashionable Amalfi coast island of Capri, and in 1949 he opened a small shop there to sell his designs. The Pucci look and his Capri pants quickly caught on with the visiting jet set.

Pucci cut his *après*-beach Capri pants without waistband or zipper, in close-fitting cotton poplin or silk shantung, inspired by Capri fishermen who rolled their pants up to their calves to avoid the waves. Pucci's choice of bright colors were the hues of his summer island.

Capri pants are classic 1950s style. Screen icon Audrey Hepburn helped to popularize them by making them part of her signature look—together with a shirt tied at the waist and flat ballet shoes. They worked their way into the influential off-duty wardrobes of idols Brigitte Bardot and Marilyn Monroe. And more than 40 years on, at the end of the twentieth century, there was a pirate pants revival.

Capri pants, popularized by screen icon Audrey Hepburn (above)
during the 1950s, still feature in the modern summer wardrobe.

COCO CHANEL
flapper dress • 1920s

Revolutionarily short and shockingly boyish, Gabrielle "Coco" Chanel's chemise dresses fell straight from the shoulders and stopped just below the knees. They came to be known as flapper dresses. They had no bodice or defined waist, just a simple scarf slung around the hips. Simplicity and comfort were the key. Chanel shaved the fuss and frills from her dresses to generate clean, modern lines: Some women softened the unforgiving silhouette with bows, hats, scarves, and costume jewelry. She used jersey for her first dresses of 1916, an unconventional but economic choice; it was traditionally used for men's underwear. *Harper's Bazaar* published a picture of one in 1916, but it was not until the 1920s that the style took off.

Chanel's straight-up-and-down dresses encapsulated the spirit of the Roaring Twenties, a decade obsessed with youth. The milliner and music hall singer from Deauville in France had created a uniform for a generation. The "bright young things" of the Jazz Age drank cocktails named Bosom Caresser and Widow's Kiss. They painted their faces and danced the Black Bottom to the strains of Django Reinhart. These "flappers"—the name appeared soon after the look, and was said to reflect their large, floppy hair bows—shocked parents and worried the New York establishment, which threatened to censor unsuitable dances.

The streamlined flapper dress looked best on a boyish, athletic, androgynous figure and was ideally worn without corsets. It was feather-light and would have felt like sportswear or underwear at the time. At last women had the freedom to dance and move. Manufacturers festooned their evening versions with beads and fringes that came alive on the dancefloor.

The chemise dress was the perfect economic fashion solution to the postwar period. Women no longer had the means or the will to buy fussy couture clothes. Couturier Lucile (the working name of Lady Duff Gordon) wrote in her book *Discretions and Indiscretions*: "The Rue de la Paix is nothing if not resourceful. It brought in the ideal of the 'boyish woman'. Here was the perfect solution to the problem. Slight figures covered with three yards of material, skirt ending just below the knees, tiny cloche hat trimmed with a band of ribbon. No woman, at least no woman in civilisation, could cost less to clothe! And best of all the women were delighted with the new presentation of themselves."

Gabrielle "Coco" Chanel in Biarritz, September 1928, wearing one of her own simple flapper dresses.

COCO CHANEL

Chanel suit • 1954

When Gabrielle "Coco" Chanel launched the tweed cardigan jacket and matching tweed knee-length skirt in the 1920s, they were revolutionary for their masculine cut and simple lines. Chanel had lived through World War I, and took soldiers as lovers, inspiring her to borrow the patch pockets and braid trim from military uniforms. She was well known for incorporating masculine elements into her designs—the tweed from sportswear and the clean silhouettes associated with menswear, for example. Wartime had given women a taste for practical, comfortable clothes previously restricted to the male domain, and Chanel played up to this with her postwar designs. The Chanel-style suit became a fashion essential.

Fast forward three decades to 1954. Chanel was in retirement, and planning a comeback, aged 71. Paris, in the full throes of curvaceous 1950s fashion, laughed condescendingly. But as always, Chanel had got it right. She brought back her light tweed suits, with their braid and ribbon trims and gilt buttons, which preempted the streamlined silhouette of the 1960s. The United States took to her suits as the comfortable uniform for the smart woman, and the suits were copied and mass-produced throughout the decade. Coco attributed her new success to being a woman designing for women, and giving them the essentials of fashion—comfort and style.

On November 22, 1963, one pink Chanel suit went down in history: the one Jacqueline Kennedy was wearing when her husband was assassinated next to her. In *America's Queen: The Life of Jacqueline Kennedy Onassis*, Sarah Bradford wrote: "She and Jack had spent a good deal of time considering her wardrobe for Texas: he wanted her to choose something simple and elegant, particularly for Dallas where, he told her, 'There are going to be all these rich Republican women ... wearing mink coats and diamond bracelets ... Show these Texans what good taste really is.' They had selected her shocking pink Chanel suit with navy trim and blouse, and matching pink pillbox hat." After the assassination: "The first [decision] was her refusal of all suggestions that she should change her skirt, stained with Jack's blood and brains. 'No,' she said fiercely, 'let them see what they've done.'"

A woman wearing a Chanel suit poses outside the Chanel boutique in Paris in 1959. The style still features on catwalks today.

COCO CHANEL

chain-handle bag • 1955

The grande dame of fashion, Gabrielle "Coco" Chanel had started out as a milliner, selling hats out of a little shop in Paris, and so it only seems natural that she should be remembered for her accessories—her larger-than-life costume jewelry and her signature chain-handled bags. In 1929 Chanel opened a boutique in her Paris salon to sell accessories: bags, belts, scarves, and jewelry. That year she had revolutionized the humble handbag by adding long shoulder straps to her jersey bags, an idea borrowed from soldiers' satchels. The woman who reputedly said: "I care more about the city street than the drawing room," had given independent women the street-wise option of hanging their bags from their shoulders. They were now free to use both hands.

Chanel launched the chain-handle bag in February 1955, the year after she came out of retirement. It was nicknamed the 2.55 to mark the date. Chanel took inspiration from the quilted linings and weights of her successful tweed cardigan suits. It was almost as if she had reached inside her suits and pulled out the bags like a magic trick. She created volume and form by quilting her bag in diamonds or herring-bone stitch, like the jackets of the dashing young stableboys she'd seen at the Deauville racetrack. She stamped eyelets into the 2.55 bag, through which she threaded a gilt chain like the ones used to weigh down the hem of her jackets. Once again, Chanel had created a luxurious fashion piece from very ordinary materials.

She stamped the lining with her insignia—three intertwined double Cs picked out in topstitch. Each bag had three compartments, the middle one designed to hold a lipstick. The flap had a further secret pocket. For day, ladies could choose a version in leather; for evening, there was a quilted bag in jersey or silk. She launched her designs in her trademark muted color palette—beige, brown, navy blue, and black. Chanel cleverly created a bag that would be instantly recognized as a Chanel, during a decade when accessories were highly prized essentials. Once again, she had scored a sartorial bull's-eye.

The Chanel chain-handle bag, with its distinctive entwined double
Cs logo, was first launched in 1955.

CHELSEA BOOT

fashion classic • 1960s

"These boots were made for walkin'," crooned Nancy Sinatra in 1966. Footwear in the 1960s was about boots: white plastic boots, Cuban-heeled boots, kinky boots, long boots, short boots, and, of course, Chelsea boots.

The Beatles—seen at the beginning of the decade as those cheeky chappies from Liverpool with their strange clothes and irresistible lyrics—set a dashing example for the 1960s generation. They were the respectable face of Mod dressing. And they topped off their androgynous skinny-legged suits with pointed boots, often with shockingly high Cuban heels, like the South American gaucho cowboys. The boots were flashy, they were streamlined, and they made you walk tall. Some were flat, others high-heeled. Some fastened with a zipper, others could pull on and pull off with elasticated side panels.

No hip cat would feel fully dressed on London's ultra-fashionable King's Road without strutting their stuff in a pair of Beatle boots, or Chelsea boots.

Photographer Robert Freeman immortalized the Beatles' boots by taking a picture of four well-worn pairs, minus their owners. These versions had pointed toes, elasticated side panels, Cuban heels, a seam running down the center and the name of each Beatle sweetly handwritten in the back of each, just showing beneath the tab.

No hip cat would feel fully dressed on London's ultra-fashionable King's Road without strutting their stuff in a pair of Beatle boots, or Chelsea boots as the elasticated versions became known. It was thanks to the Fab Four that ankle boots for men came back into fashion. In fact, the Beatle boots looked a little like boots worn in Victorian times.

Teeny-bop hysteria mounted and Beatlemania mushroomed. London's *Evening Standard* dubbed 1963 as "The Year of the Beatles"—the world scrutinized, discussed, and copied everything about the world's favorite boy band, from their girlfriends to their footwear. The *Daily Mirror* summed it up perfectly in the same year: "Boots with everything."

A pair of brown Chelsea boots from the 1970s. They had become essential footwear for fashion-followers in the previous decade.

KURT COBAIN

fashion icon • 1967–1994

"Load up on guns and bring your friends, It's fun to lose, And to pretend," went the lyrics of Nirvana's legendary anthem, "Smells Like Teen Spirit." Kurt Cobain, lead singer of band Nirvana, was the pretty boy of grunge music, the punk and heavy metal hybrid that came out of Seattle. He captured the world's youth with his good looks and laidback style. He shocked with his drug-taking. And he blew his brains out with a shotgun in a Seattle greenhouse. Cobain took grunge music into the mainstream: *Rolling Stone* magazine called him the "icon of the 1990s."

With grunge music came the grunge look, and the kids on the street took it up in the late 1980s and early 1990s. It borrowed from skate, surf, and thrash-metal styles. It was the absolute antidote to the power dressing of the 1980s. And it was accessible. Anyone with a pinch of attitude and youth on their side could wear it. Ripped and bleached jeans, and shorts cut off just below the knee. Flowery dresses with leggings, leather boots, and army surplus. Punk T-shirts, thrift shop clothing, shirts over T-shirts. And all this was mixed, matched, rumpled, crumpled and layered. It was customized, torn, and mismatched. It wasn't what you wore—it was the way you wore it. Grunge was about antifashion.

Young fashion designer Marc Jacobs listened to Cobain's lyrics and bought a plaid shirt. He looked at the rockstar's wife, Courtney Love (who had a passion for couture), and watched how kids were dressing on the streets. And he put it on the catwalk. "Here we are now, entertain us," rasps Cobain in "Smells Like Teen Spirit"—and Jacobs did just that. In 1993 he did lace, stripes, fruit prints, laddered tights, and 1930s dresses, all teamed with army boots and belly chains. It was dubbed the grunge look, and it took off.

The grunge look was the absolute antidote to the power dressing of the late 1980s. And it was accessible. Anyone with a pinch of attitude and youth could wear it.

But only for a while. Donna Karan did her take on grunge for DKNY. Anna Sui followed suit. Ralph Lauren tried a more sedate version. But the ridiculous designer grunge look was short-lived. Why should we buy the thrift store look with designer price tag?, wondered the fashion pack. And by the time the bullets had left Cobain's gun in 1994, grunge fashion was dead.

Come As You Are: the king of grunge performs with Nirvana.

Designer grunge was a shortlived experiment.

ANDRÉ COURRÈGES

Space Age collection • 1964

In 1962 John Glenn became the first man in space, and from then on, intergalactic fever gripped a generation obsessed with looking forward rather than back. At the epicenter of the sartorial space race was French designer André Courrèges, an ex-civil engineer. His 1964 Space Age collection blew the critics away with his vision of the future. It became one of the most influential looks of the 1960s and set the tone for the decade.

A small all-white and chrome showroom. The insistent drumming of a jazz rhythm. Short skirts worn with strange flat white plastic boots. Clothes sliced into uncompromisingly architectural square-cut shapes. This was what bowled over the audience at Courrèges's fashion show. His geometric, stark silhouettes looked so new because they were so simple. Courrèges used heavy fabric so that the pieces would keep their clean shapes. He denounced the stiletto, pronounced the miniskirt couture, and put young sporty models in helmets and sharply cut wigs. *Vogue* commented in 1965. "A question everyone is asking in Paris. A catch phrase repeated *ad nauseam*. Is Courrèges wearable? Do you really think Courrèges is wearable? Can one show oneself in the street dressed in creations designed for the year 2000?"

This was the first time that Courrèges had really come into his own. In 1961 he had left the atelier of Christobal Balenciaga, where he worked as an assistant, to set up on his own with his future wife, Coqueline. But it took him until 1964 to mature into his own style. After that, there was no stopping him.

The Courrèges philosophy was that clothes should hang away from the body rather than cling to the natural curves. His specialties included short, triangular "trapeze line" shift dresses, and long, slim trousers slit at the seam to fit over the shoes. He placed tunics over trousers and ran up pantsuits in white or silver. Courrèges's bizarre glasses were all white, with just a slit to enable the wearer to see.

His white boots and short, clean dresses became a sign of the times for the 1960s generation. And in answer to *Vogue*'s question, women did dare to show themselves wearing Courrèges, or Courrèges style. His Space Age collection was copied and copied and copied again.

A day dress by Courrèges, February 1967. His futuristic, Space Age
designs proved an unlikely step forward for couture.

JAMES DEAN

fashion icon • 1931–1955

Forever immortalized as that pretty, pretty boy, filmstar James Dean starred in just three films before crashing and dying in his sparkling new Porsche Spyder. His car was customized with the painted words "the little Bastard," his nickname for it. He was just 24 years old. It was 1955, and the filming for *Giant*, his third and final major movie, hadn't yet finished. Ironically, earlier in the same year, Dean had made a highway safety commercial in which he said: "Take it easy driving. The life you save might be mine."

Dying was the best career move that Jimmy Dean ever made. The man who had been dubbed the next Marlon Brando instantly became a screen legend and a teenage cult hero. The fan mail poured in. As François Truffaut wrote in *Arts* magazine a year after the actor's death, "In James Dean, today's youth discovers itself." Dean posthumously inspired more films than he actually starred in alive.

James Dean's first film, *East of Eden*, was released in 1955, and it made him a star overnight. His roles explored dissatisfied youth and teenage angst. His onscreen uniform of T-shirt and jeans became

James Dean's on-screen uniform of T-shirt and jeans became accepted dress for teenagers who wanted to appear rebellious.

accepted dress for teenagers who wanted to appear rebellious. They loved his cheeky stetson worn cocked back on his head, his black leather jacket, and his blood-red windbreaker from *Rebel Without a Cause*, copies of which sold for months after his death. They dreamed of driving fast cars. They copied his dangling cigarette, sideburns, and slouch. At the time, the white T-shirt still had associations with men's underwear, jeans were still worn as workmen's overalls, and leather jackets were associated with thugs and wild motorcycle boys. It was a winning bad-boy adolescent formula.

Jeans and T-shirts became the rebel youth uniform of the 1950s, the mainstream unisex standard of the 1970s, and a classic combination that men and women returned to in the 1980s. Dean, immortalized forever as the king of cool, had unwittingly set a trend.

The original rebel without a cause, James Dean, wearing the jacket and jeans combination that inspired future generations.

Marlene Dietrich wears a masculine-style trousersuit by Coco Chanel, 1933. Her daring style both shocked and inspired.

MARLENE DIETRICH

fashion icon • 1901–1992

Nicknamed "the best dressed man in Hollywood," film legend Marlene Dietrich had the nerve to go where most women wouldn't. She strutted the streets in a pantsuit. Women sometimes wore pants at the beach or in the evening, but never as part of a suit during the daytime. When the German actress visited France, the Paris police chief was so scandalized by her attire that he asked her to leave the city.

In the early 1930s, Dietrich arrived in the United States, where the famous Paramount studio costume designer, Travis Banton, took her under his wing. He groomed her and dressed her, onscreen and off. She lost weight, painted her eyebrows into high arches, and became every inch the star. From 1933 Marlene favored relaxed-cut pantsuits with wide padded shoulders. She teamed them with mannish shirts, cufflinks, ties, and a hat worn rakishly on one side of her head. Dietrich often topped a razor-sharp jacket with lavish furs.

Paradoxically, Marlene's carefully cut masculine clothes only emphasized her feminine elegance and chic. Her pants drew attention to her famous legs, yet tantalizingly veiled them. You couldn't miss her.

In her day, people regarded the husky-voiced, iconic Dietrich as a woman in man's clothing. Dietrich made no secret of her bisexuality, which was very daring for the times. So when she wore a pantsuit in public, she scandalized because she seemed to be openly flaunting her sexual freedom. She used pantsuits to challenge sexual mores, both on the screen and on the street. For her 1930 American screen debut in *Morocco*, she wore a black top hat, white tie, and tails. Marlene swaggered like a man in her suit, pulled on a cigarette, and planted a kiss smack-bang on the lips of a woman in the audience. The publicity slogan for the movie read: "The Woman even Women can Adore." Dietrich was a screen goddess, Hollywood royalty, at the height of cinema mania, so she could, and did, behave as she pleased.

Although women copied the Marlene look, in reality not many were prepared to go the whole way and wear a pantsuit as severe as Dietrich's. The fashion didn't really take off until the 1960s, when Yves Saint Laurent introduced his version, Le Smoking. But Marlene's pantsuits began the blurring of the boundaries between appropriate masculine and feminine dress.

CHRISTIAN DIOR

the New Look • 1947

Paris, the Avenue Montaigne, 1947. Christian Dior's first show. The models come flying through the crowded room, swinging their wasp waists and knocking over ashtrays with their sweeping ballerina skirts. The new silhouette caused a sensation and a scandal. Dior called it the Corolle line—named for the way his skirts billowed out from tiny waistlines like a flower's corolla of petals—but *Harper's Bazaar* fashion editor Carmel Snow dubbed it the New Look, and it stuck. Dior had made his mark, much to the delight of textile magnate Marcel Boussac, who had plucked the designer from the couture house of Lucien Lelong and offered to finance a couture house of his own.

Dior gave women dresses to dream about. But the sheer excess of his wide-pleated skirts was shockingly extreme. The thrifty postwar generation was still reeling from poverty and scarce basic materials, including fabric. In Britain, clothing was still rationed. Politicians condemned this new extravagance—but Dior had opened the floodgates of temptation.

British *Vogue* reported in April 1947: "Christian Dior ... is the new name in Paris. With his first collection he not only shot into fame, but retrieved the general situation by reviving interest in a somewhat uninspired season .... Dior uses fabric lavishly in skirts—15 yards in a woollen day dress, 25 yards in short taffeta evening dress. He pads these pleated skirts with stiff cambric; builds corsets and busts into the dresses so that they practically stand alone." The New Look ushered in an hourglass silhouette that was all woman: small waists, wide hips, full busts, sloping shoulders, and wide skirts. It suggested womanhood, motherhood, curves developed from larders stocked with food, limitless bank balances, and a brave new world. It was the ultimate contrast to wartime death, destruction, and hunger. And women wanted it.

Those who could afford to bought the real thing from the 1947 Dior collection, such as the pink and black Le Bar suit. Those who couldn't sewed panels onto their hems, and pulled apart and reconstructed their wartime dresses. When the manufacturers reproduced the New Look for the mass market, Dior's success was confirmed. It is fair to say that the mean, slim, wartime silhouette had already slightly softened, but Dior, with his decadent sweeping dresses, helped to fast-forward fashion into a new decade.

The swinging skirt and nipped-in waist introduced by Christian Dior
in 1947 created a dramatic new silhouette.

DUNGAREES

fashion classic • 1939–1945

In Britain the Women's Land Army recruited the fairer sex for agricultural work while the men were away fighting during World War II. The Land Girls, in their blue dungarees, green sweaters, corduroy breeches, and canvas gaiters, set to work sowing the seed and tilling the soil for the war effort. They brought in the harvest and plowed the fields, using horses because of petrol rationing. They became rat-catchers, milkmaids, and shepherdesses. They turned soccer pitches and golf courses into farmland. Their Timber Corps, known as the "Lumber Jills," felled and planted trees. And they even had their own song: "Back to the Land, we must all lend a hand, To the farms and the fields we must go, There's a job to be done, Though we can't fire a gun, We can still do our bit with the hoe. When your muscles are strong, You will soon get along. And you'll think that country life's grand; We're all needed now, We must all speed the plough, So come with us—back to the Land." They were told to "Dig for Victory," and they did.

The word dungarees comes from the Hindi *dungri*, which means a coarse blue calico used for sails: When a sail became torn and storm-ravaged, the sailors would cut it up to make pants. Dungaree pants, with their bib-tops and shoulder straps, were

Dungarees drove the men wild: Marilyn Monroe once claimed that a woman in overalls was as provocative as a woman in her underwear.

worn by the rural poor and workmen in the early twentieth century, but the two world wars marked the first time that women slipped into these masculine garments. While the factory workers took to wearing overalls, sleeveless dungarees came to be associated with the field wear of the Land Girls.

Wartime marked the turning point when women were allowed to wear the pants—but of course for work only. After World War II, they were expected to go back and keep house in pretty little dresses. But some grew fond of their practical, emancipated dungarees. And they drove the men wild—Marilyn Monroe once claimed that a woman in overalls was as provocative as a woman in her underwear. In the 1940s and 1950s, just like denim jeans, dungarees became fashionable in their own right.

Land Army girls in dungarees in July 1940. Women had rarely worn such practical clothes before World War II.

SALVATORE FERRAGAMO
wedge and platform • 1930s

Salvatore Ferragamo, shoemaker to stars and royalty, set up a Hollywood custom-made shoe business in the 1920s. By 1939 he had salons in Florence, Milan, and Rome. Ferragamo is credited with inventing the wedge shoe, and is famous for his flamboyant platform shoes.

By the late 1930s, shorter skirts and wide shoulder pads fueled a demand for heavier shoes to balance the exaggerated silhouette. Ferragamo came up with the wedge sole. Wedges had already been used for rubber bathing shoes and beach sandals, but Ferragamo made them chic. His wedge was a continuous platform sole that ran from the toe up to the heel in a solid triangular block.

The Duchess Visconti di Modrone was the first woman to wear Ferragamo wedges. In 1938 the designer made brown leather cork-covered wedge-heel shoes for Maria Jose, queen of Italy (she reigned for only 27 days). And Greta Garbo loved his simple black leather shoes, with their scarlet wedge heels. Ferragamo was the darling of the stars.

Roger Vivier is credited with making the first platform shoe, but Ferragamo took it to new, innovative heights and made it fashionable. Whereas a wedge heel was a solid triangle so the foot sloped downward, with the platform, the front of the foot was also elevated. Singer and dancer Carmen Miranda had a passion for Ferragamo's platforms. She was photographed posing with 40 pairs in the late 1930s—her most memorable pair was gold with a platform sole of gilded glass mosaic.

Ferragamo was the master of invention: He was not scared of pushing the boundaries when it came to materials and construction. In 1938 he invented a canvas sandal with a wooden platform sole that was hinged for walking. Wartime shortages encouraged him to experiment with straw, hemp, rubber, paper, and even fish skin. And he set a trend for wood and cork heels.

Ferragamo's reputation still stands as one of the most innovative shoemakers of the twentieth century. His theatrical wedge and platform designs fueled the imagination of shoe enthusiasts all around the globe.

Platform sandal with padded kid upper and cork sole by Ferragamo,
1938. The Italian shoemaker took platforms to new heights.

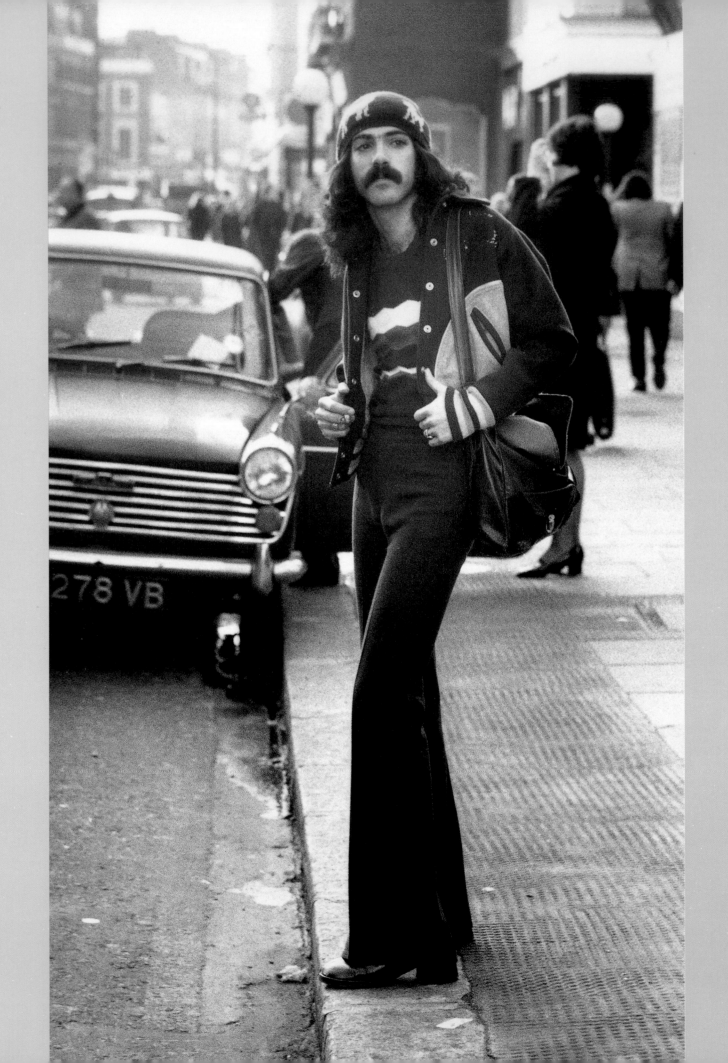

FLARES

fashion classic • 1960s

Hip and streetwise? Fashion faux pas? What is the appeal of the pant-bottoms that flap around the ankles and flare out from the knee?

Bell-bottoms were traditionally worn by sailors in the British Navy—white for summer and navy blue for winter. But it was in the late 1960s and early 1970s that flares really caught on. At the time, everything seemed more exaggerated. Young men and women grew their hair, let down their hemlines, elongated their collars, and raised their shoes with platform soles. Flared trousers became universal—flared jeans, flared suit pants, and flared velvet loon pants. Hippies danced in fields in them and businessmen talked shop in them. Urban African-Americans pioneered the funk-style flares of the 1970s, cut tight over the hips, crotch, and thighs in sensual fabric. Funk was about sex appeal and looking smart, whereas flower power was about looking scruffy.

Barbara Hulanicki, founder of cult 1960s British boutique Biba, wrote in her book, *From A to Biba*: "One day a huge black limousine parked by the spiky railings outside the shop. A very strange group got out and sauntered in. All, female and male, were wearing the most exaggerated flared trousers. Ours were flared, but not as much as these. For once I felt upstaged! The tops of those pants were so tight and so low on the hip they looked as if they might slip off ... It was Sonny and Cher." These were hipsters, flares that stopped at the hip rather than the waist and fastened with a wide belt.

Flares have a way of slipping back into fashion. During the 1980s in England, Manchester football supporters wore them to matches. For fans of Manchester pop groups the Stone Roses and the Happy Mondays they were a status symbol—the bigger and baggier the better. With the 1990s came the mainstream boot cut, which kicked out in a flare from the knee. It worked well for jeans, corduroys, and black stretch trousers. Flares, it seems, are here to stay.

Knitted skullcap and flared pants: a British hippy in full uniform in
the early 1970s, but flares had been around decades earlier (above).

FRED PERRY SHIRT

fashion classic • 1940s

English tennis player Fred Perry made sporting history when he won three consecutive Wimbledon singles titles from 1934 to 1936. Remarkably, he remains the first and last Englishman to win Wimbledon to date. The Brits were proud.

During the 1940s, former soccer player Tibby Wegner came up with an idea to cash in on the dapper sportsman's style. Together, they designed a toweling sweatband emblazoned with the words "Fred Perry." Then came the Fred Perry white three-button pique tennis shirt, with a new logo a laurel wreath (Perry's own idea of a tobacco pipe was, not surprisingly, turned down). Marketing was easy—they gave the shirts away to the major tennis stars and TV cameramen. Perry, now a commentator, wore his on early television. It worked. The major sports stores queued up to buy the shirt. The next move was colored Fred Perry shirts, and the definitive stripes on the collar.

Little did Perry know that his well-cut shirts were to become more associated with soccer than tennis. They became cult items of British working class youth from the 1960s onward. The Mods wore them with "hiphanger" hipster pants in the early 1960s. At the beginning of the 1970s, skinheads converged at soccer matches in their Fred Perry shirts, Dr. Martens boots, and faded Levi's Sta-Prest jeans, looking for a fight. Then the Fred Perry shirt passed to the suede-heads, with their slightly longer hair, tight corduroy trousers, and tonic suits.

It was not until the end of the 1970s that Manchester subculture paid the greatest homage to Fred. Youths dressing in a chic casual style, wearing sportswear from head to toe, christened themselves the "Perries" after their Fred Perry shirts. In turn, the Perries influenced a new subcultural group in the early 1980s, the "casuals," who hit the football terraces wearing Burberry, Pringle, and Lacoste (René Lacoste was originally a tennis star, like Perry).

During the 1990s, some 60 years after Perry won Wimbledon, Britpop stars continued to wear his shirts. And when *i-D* magazine went to Manchester to report on the "Scally" house music scene, one local sneered, "We're not called Scallies ... Scallies don't exist around here, it's Perry Boys, the Boys or Firms ... Scallies [is] a dickhead word." Perry culture was still going strong.

Dapper sportsman Fred Perry gave his name to a shirt now more closely associated with soccer terraces than lawn tennis.

JOHN GALLIANO

Les Incroyables degree show • 1984

John Galliano is a fashion great of the twenty-first century. He is now at the top of his field. But how did it all start? His big break was his 1984 St. Martin's School of Art degree show, named Les Incroyables, the first time Galliano's talent went on public display. In the audience was businesswoman and fashion aficionado Joan Burstein, of London designer store Browns. She singled Galliano out, took a risk, and bought the entire eight-piece collection, which she displayed in her shop window. The collection sold out. Galliano received first-class honors. And bingo—a star was born. Just two years later, Galliano was crowned British Designer of the Year.

What was so special about Galliano's collection? Les Incroyables captivated the audience in a flurry of history, theater, and the romance of the French Revolution. Galliano had researched French history between 1792 and 1802—the decade bridging the falling of the monarchy and Napoleon's rise to power. He learned about the wild groups of French youth on the barricades, in clothing that was dashingly duel-slashed and torn: tight trousers for men that left little to the imagination, and daringly revealing diaphanous muslin dresses for women. Taking this as inspiration, Galliano dressed boys and girls as swashbuckling, debonair romantics. He also tapped into the New Romantic undercurrent coursing through the London club scene, to which he was no stranger.

Les Incroyables was not just theater. Galliano successfully experimented with ways to drape and cut fabric, creating new loose silhouettes.

His Les Incroyables women wore skinny trousers with voluminous organdie shirts tied in a large cravat at the neck. The boys wore patchwork waistcoats with fluid jersey skirts. He designed loose wrapped pants, and wide coats like capes. And this was all topped off with red, white, and blue rosettes and powdered hair, which gave off short talc puffs as the models strutted their stuff.

Les Incroyables was not just theater. Galliano successfully experimented with ways to drape and cut fabric, creating new loose silhouettes. The man who would become famous for his fluid, bias-cut dresses, and go on to design for Givenchy and Dior, was launched.

Right from his 1984 degree show, John Galliano has always brought a great sense of theater to his fashion shows.

GRETA GARBO - Metro Goldwyn - Mayer

GRETA GARBO

fashion icon • 1905–1990

Swedish-born actress Greta Garbo entranced cinema audiences of the 1920s and 1930s with her icy good looks and husky voice. In 1932 *Vanity Fair* called her: "The strange and angular siren of the movies, the legend of the studios ... this fair Scandinavian, whose every movement is instinct with beauty, whose name evokes mystery, whose image evokes desire." Women particularly were enthralled with her distant beauty and *femme fatale* movie roles, and, at this time, Hollywood was the major influence on mainstream fashion.

With the help of MGM's famed costume designer, Adrian, and her own natural sense of style, Greta Garbo made her mark. She was already well versed in the power of image, having worked as a millinery assistant and model in Sweden. Garbo fans slavishly copied her bobbed hair. But it was with her romantic onscreen hats that the actress had the most influence. She popularized the slouch felt cloche hat in *A Woman of Affairs* (1929); the velvet Eugénie hat, worn tilted over one eye, in *Romance* (1930); the pillbox hat from *As You Desire Me* (1932); the wide-brimmed hat from *Queen Christina* (1933); the bejeweled skullcap from *Mata Hari* (1931).

All it took was for Garbo to star in The Kiss *in 1929, wearing a sporty Basque-style beret, and the beret became fashionable.*

All it took was for Garbo to star in *The Kiss* in 1929, wearing a sporty Basque-style beret, and the beret became fashionable. *The Kiss* was Garbo's last silent film for MGM. She played the wife of a silk merchant, tried for her husband's murder after adulterously kissing an 18-year-old. The pliable circular beret, with its little stalk on top and band that grips the head, was traditionally worn by Basque peasants, but can be traced back to ancient Greece and Rome.

Vogue included a beret on its pages in 1930, with the caption: "When you sail into the harbour at Arcachon, you will be wearing Worth's yachting costume 'Ocean', with woollen trousers, flannel jacket, striped shirt and blue beret." And then in the late 1960s, the beret ricocheted back into fashion thanks to another movie star—Faye Dunaway in *Bonnie and Clyde* (1967).

Greta Garbo in As You Desire Me, *April 1932. The actress popularized many styles of hats, but especially the beret and slouch hat.*

JEAN-PAUL GAULTIER

bustier • 1990

Jean-Paul Gaultier blurred the boundaries between decency and indecency—outerwear and underwear—when he reintroduced the bustier. The bustier, or corset, with its shoulder straps and tight bodice, was originally worn as underwear to shape the female torso during the nineteenth century. Women went back to it in the 1950s to help them achieve the obligatory nipped-in waist and voluptuous bust. Yet the corset was always hidden away in a bedroom or boudoir, for the eyes of the intimate and the imagination of the prurient.

By the body-worshipping 1980s, bustiers, bodices, and corsets were a defunct commodity in terms of practical underwear. But soon they were blatantly displayed in public—on the catwalks, in the clubs, and on the street. Women now wore them as outerwear, with a pantsuit during the day, or in the evening with a skirt or pair of pants. Thanks to Gaultier, the bustier had gone mainstream.

It was Gaultier's childhood fascination with Le Moulin Rouge and his grandmother's corsets that led him as an adult to readdress the bustier. He first put corsets on the catwalk in 1983 as part of his La Dadaïste collection. And from then on, the corset became a Gaultier trademark.

Gaultier promoted the corset as outerwear in its own right. He took the sexual mystique out of the bustier, placing it on the catwalk for all to see. If anything, wearing a corset in public now meant sexual power. The torso, hardened and molded by a bustier with its conical stitched breast cups, was like body armor on display, a sign of strength.

No one could have embodied these ideas better than Madonna. She used Gaultier's corsets as a symbol of independence rather than sexual repression. When she asked Gaultier to design the outfits for her highly charged 1990 Blonde Ambition tour, he took the corset as his dominant theme. Madonna tantalized her fans in a raunchy gold corset and fishnet stockings. A corset Gaultier found in his grandmother's cupboard inspired her flesh-pink-quilted satin bustier with pointed 1950s-style cups. But over in Rome, the Vatican was not amused. It condemned the tour as "satanic" and excommunicated Madonna from the Catholic church. Gaultier had lived up to his nickname—the *enfant terrible*.

Madonna shows off Gaultier's infamous ice-pink bustier on her 1990
Blonde Ambition tour.

JEAN-PAUL GAULTIER

male skirt • 1985

Can a man wear a skirt, but still retain his masculinity? That was the question that teased the audience of Jean-Paul Gaultier's 1985 menswear show. He called it "And God Created Man" (a pastiche of the Brigitte Bardot screen hit *And God Created Woman*)—and he put men in skirts. Well, they looked like skirts. They were really pant legs that wrapped over each other, like Thai fishermen's pants, so that the legs appeared to be joined. Gaultier's inspiration came from a pair of Bermuda shorts by Jacques Esterel, and the work of fashion stylist Ray Petri, who dressed tough-looking male models in skirts in 1984. And once Gaultier had started the skirt revolution, he couldn't stop. He put men in sarongs and pinstriped apron-fronted pants, and he started to show off his own legs in a kilt, teaming it with his signature striped sailor top.

Gaultier broke sartorial taboos and challenged male sexual stereotypes. Of course, he was criticized for making men look ridiculous. In the 1980s, women dominated boardrooms in their power suits, relaxed in ripped 501s, and marched the streets in pantsuits. Women had appropriated traditionally male dress, the designer argued—so why shouldn't it work the other way round? Gaultier thought that items of clothing should not be affiliated with one sex or the other. He wanted people to regard the skirt as a piece of men's clothing in its own right, like the Scottish kilt or the Indian lunghi. And to push the point home—and infuriate his critics—he put male models on the catwalk in revealing lace skirts, while the girls smoked pipes.

> Gaultier wanted people to regard the skirt as a piece of men's clothing in its own right, like the Scottish kilt or the Indian lunghi.

The *Face* magazine reported in a Gaultier interview in 1986: "The first time he showed men in skirts, the 30-strong French *Vogue* staff stood up and, in a flurry of Saint Laurent, made a mass exit, closely followed by the retinues of *Marie Claire* and French *Elle*. [Gaultier said:] 'I was slated in the French press for designing clothes for homosexuals and hairdressers! It took them two years to accept my statement that Prince Charles is not the only real man to wear a skirt.'" Gaultier didn't quite succeed in putting the man on the street in a skirt. But he did get him thinking about one of fashion's final taboos.

RUDI GERNREICH

monokini • 1964

The pope banned it. A Detroit department store received a bomb threat because of it. St. Tropez's mayor threatened to use helicopters to spot immoral topless sunbathers. What was all the fuss about? It was United States-based Austrian designer Rudi Gernreich's topless swimsuit, or monokini, of 1964.

The costume stopped at the ribcage, like high-waisted bikini bottoms. Only a thin strap ran up the center of the body and around the neck like a skinny halterneck. Breasts were on full display. And the United States was scandalized. Gernreich had felt that 1964 was too early to launch the costume, but Susanne Kirtland of *Look* magazine persuaded him to make one for a fashion shoot. In the end, a prostitute modeled it on a beach in the Bahamas, and the photographer shot it from the back. Gernreich had never considered putting the piece into production, but when buyers started clamoring for it, he gave in. Three thousand monokinis sold.

The designer claimed that his aim was to liberate the body and celebrate movement with his costume, rather than draw attention to the bared breasts. He regarded breasts as just another part of the body, rather than something to be hidden away.

Gernreich's training as a dancer and mortuary worker instilled a fascination with the body. He freed women from the boned 1950s-style swimsuits of the time, which pulled in the stomach and reshaped the bust. Instead, he offered daring jersey costumes that revealed every curve. Function and freedom were his buzzwords.

> *Gernreich was a pioneer, a man ahead of his time. He challenged the world to question why a woman should not bare her breasts on the beach like a man.*

Gernreich was a pioneer, a man ahead of his time. *Harper's Bazaar* described him in 1964 as being "Famous for avant-garde, drop-dead clothes that look newly invented." His designs were forerunners to the bra-burning 1970s and women's sexual liberation. He challenged the world to question why a woman should not bare her breasts on the beach like a man. Gernreich anticipated an era when women would sunbathe topless quite openly. And he was right.

Rudi Gernreich's topless swimsuit, from about 1964. His daring design shocked the world—but 3,000 monokinis sold.

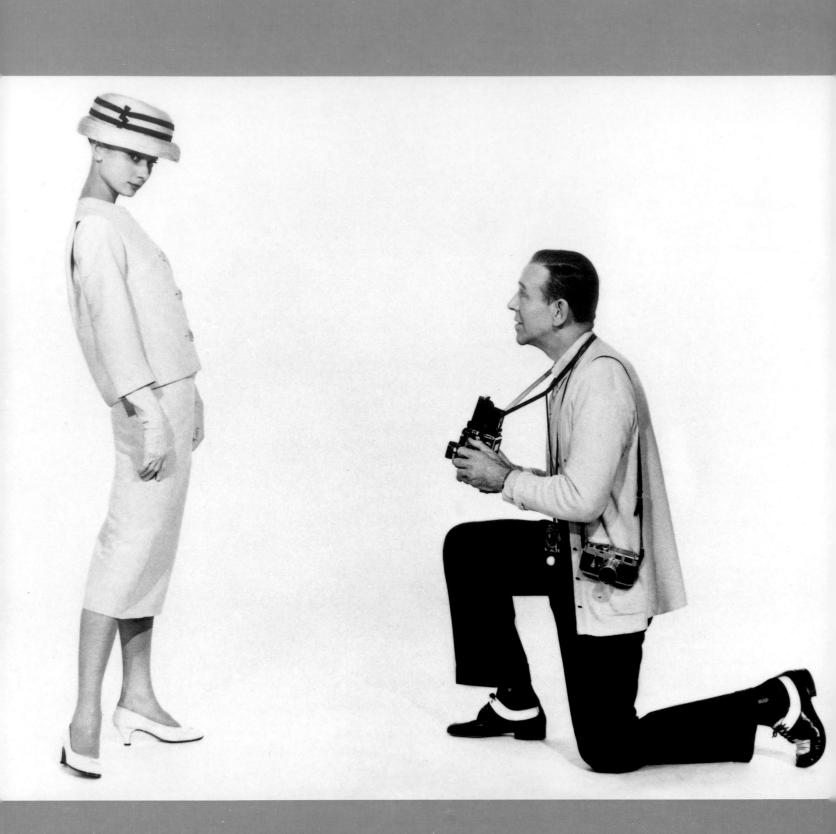

HUBERT DE GIVENCHY

designs for *Funny Face* • 1957

"Think pink! think pink! when you shop for summer clothes. Think pink! think pink! if you want that *quelque chose*. Red is dead, blue is through, Green's obscene, brown's taboo," went the lyrics for the 1957 screen musical *Funny Face*. A photographer (inspired by Richard Avedon and played by Fred Astaire) discovers a girl working in a bookshop (Audrey Hepburn) and catapults her into the spotlight as a fashion model. The film was the perfect vehicle for dressing Audrey up in beautiful couture clothes. Hepburn called on Paris couturier Hubert de Givenchy for her character's wardrobe (Hollywood costume designer Edith Head dressed the rest of the cast). Givenchy had opened his couture house in 1952, with Balenciaga as mentor, and was known for his elegant, pared-down designs and youthful separates. The *Funny Face* costumes were a huge success, and, as a result, Givenchy shared an Academy Award nomination with Edith Head.

> The "Audrey Look" mushroomed. Young copycat Hepburns bounced along city streets in flat shoes, big glasses, black turtlenecks, and ballerina skirts.

Hepburn entranced *Funny Face* audiences with her coltish good looks and elegant style. In a flower market, she wears Givenchy's wide-skirted dress, embroidered with roses inspired by nineteenth-century paintings. She clutches a large bunch of balloons in a capped-sleeved black dress with a wide skirt. She saunters down steps in a knockout scarlet dress, but then slums it in slim black beatnik pants, a headscarf, and a black turtleneck. She goes fishing in a cropped top, cigarette pants, and a wide straw hat.

Funny Face marked the beginning of the official Givenchy–Hepburn collaboration (he had designed some costumes for her in the earlier film *Sabrina*, though Edith Head took the credit). Givenchy went on to dress Audrey on and off screen. And together they created a style icon. She captured the hearts of the world with her elfin face and languid fashion model frame—looks startlingly different from the curvaceous blonde bombshells of the day, the Monroes and Bardots. The "Audrey Look" mushroomed. Young copycat Hepburns bounced along city streets in flat shoes, big glasses, black turtlenecks, and ballerina skirts. Hepburn was the biggest walking, talking advertisement for Givenchy's designs. She said: "I was born to wear them."

Audrey Hepburn with Fred Astaire in the 1956 movie Funny Face.
Hepburn wears a design by Hubert de Givenchy.

Halston surrounded by models wearing his classic, fluid designs,
pictured in American Vogue, *1972.*

HALSTON

jersey dress • 1970s

Handsome, talented Roy Halston Frowick charmed America's Cat Pack and coaxed them into his slinky jersey dresses. And they loved him for it. Like Coco Chanel, he worked as a milliner before producing his first clothing collection in 1966. And like Chanel, simplicity, elegance, and function were his hallmarks. Which is why *Womenswear Daily* (1976) nicknamed him Mr. Clean.

Halston worked hard and played hard. He regularly partied until the sun came up at legendary New York nightclub Studio 54 with his disco diva clients Liza Minnelli and Bianca Jagger. He realized that, in the 1970s, the feelgood factor was as important as looking good. He freed women from heavily constructed couture clothes. Halston's clients wanted dresses they could walk in, run in, and, most importantly, dance till dawn in. As he said: "I am giving women what they want. Women want to be comfortable and they want to look sexy. It's as simple as that."

Flattering the female figure was Halston's art. His fluid dresses transformed clients into feline glamor pusses like 1930s Hollywood stars. "His whole point was to sculpt a woman's body so if there was a part she didn't like, he could hide it, and the parts she liked, he showed. For me, he liked my shoulders, so he would hang everything from them," said his muse Liza Minnelli.

Halston was renowned for his full-length jersey halterneck dresses and toga dresses. He coaxed the fabric into a bodice and up over one shoulder like the robes of a Greek goddess. Halston's secret weapon was to cut his silk and rayon jersey on the bias. The fabric would then drape diaphanously over the body. He used plain colors to reveal the body shape underneath.

The twists and layers that looked so simple on the body were impossibly complicated to construct. Taking his cue from 1930s designer Madeleine Vionnet, Halston challenged himself to remove as many linings, seams, and zippers as he could. Instead of creating form with pattern pieces, he preferred knots or twists. And rather than sketches, he used folds of paper origami to realize his ideas. His tube dress was a single piece of fabric, spiraled round the body.

In Halston, America's jet set of the 1970s had at last found some home-grown fashion talent of its own. Who needed Paris when you had Halston in New York?

HALSTON

pillbox hat • 1961

When First Lady Jacqueline, wife of John F. Kennedy, needed a hat to wear for the 1961 presidential inauguration, she turned to milliner Halston. He came up with a new take on the pillbox hat. Greta Garbo had first set a trend for the pillbox in 1932 when she wore one in the film *As You Desire Me*. Halston borrowed the basic shape and adapted it to sit over Jackie's large bouffant hairstyle. She wore it perched back, rather than pulled forward, and it was an instant hit. The elegant, shockingly simple design was perfect for a First Lady who loathed wearing hats but felt compelled to do her duty.

Jackie was already a style icon. She had good looks and youth on her side, and drew attention to both by choosing elegant clothing and accessories. Halston ran the high-profile custom millinery salon at department store Bergdorf Goodman, having learned his trade with New York milliner Lilly Daché. What both Halston and Kennedy shared was a love of clean lines and simple shapes. Where

Halston shared a special relationship with the First Lady—his head was exactly the same size as hers, so he could fit her hats while she was on the other side of the globe.

other designers binged on feathers and fuss, Halston believed that less was decidedly more. His minimalist designs suited the dominating beehives and backcombed big hair of the 1960s. Jackie's fully coiffed hair measured an astounding 24 inches (60cm) in diameter. Halston shared a special relationship with the First Lady—his head was exactly the same size as hers, so he could fit her hats while she was on the other side of the globe.

Jackie Kennedy's very public endorsement of Halston as a milliner was a turning point in his career. The pillbox became part of the First Lady's uniform, and soon the world's women were clamoring for a hat just like Jackie's. Halston's became a bestseller. Manufacturers rushed to copy it in wool, silk, fur, and straw. When Jackie reached up to grab her pillbox in the wind, accidentally denting it, milliners even copied the dent. Halston's hats started to appear on the pages of *Vogue* and *Harper's Bazaar*. And when legendary fashion doyenne and ex-American *Vogue* editor Diana Vreeland dubbed him the "greatest hatmaker in the world," Halston knew he had made it. He would soon turn his hand to designing clothes, too.

Princess Diana in a pillbox hat, June 1985. The style was popularized in the 1960s by America's own princess, Jacqueline Kennedy.

KATHARINE HAMNETT

slogan T-shirt • 1984

"Big words on even bigger T-shirts are definitely this summer's thing," claimed British magazine *Smash Hits* in 1984. White T-shirts were all over the U.K. that summer, displaying slogans in bold black capitals, from STOP KILLING WHALES and FRANKIE SAYS ARM THE UNEMPLOYED to WOMEN ARE ANGRY. Why open your mouth to shout when your clothes can do it for you?

It all started with Katharine Hamnett, who designed T-shirts as political and environmental protest statements. She set a major fashion trend. She married the power of clothes with the power of the written word, and in the summer of 1984, young Brits went about their business looking like animated placards from a street demonstration. She didn't mince her words—BAN POLLUTION, HEROIN FREE ZONE, and WORLDWIDE NUCLEAR BAN NOW. The famous 1984 photograph of Hamnett shaking hands with prime minister Margaret Thatcher in a provocative T-shirt that read 58% DON'T WANT PERSHING stuck in the minds of the nation. And it fueled her sales. The bold slogan T-shirt in Hamnett's distinctive typeface became a sign of the times.

The bold slogan T-shirt in Hamnett's distinctive typeface became a sign of the times. Why open your mouth to shout when your clothes can do it for you?

While Hamnett's T-shirts were about fashion with a conscience (some of the profits were donated to good causes), the high street, the music industry, and T-shirt manufacturers pillaged her design for their own means. She claimed she knew the T-shirts would be copied, but didn't mind because her slogan messages would reach more people. She may not, however, have anticipated that her T-shirt saying CHOOSE LIFE was to mutate into the teenybopper's CHOOSE WHAM!. In the charts that summer, the band Frankie Goes to Hollywood shot to number one with "Relax." And soon, T-shirts emblazoned with FRANKIE SAYS RELAX were hot street wear for the fashionable.

Hamnett received the British Fashion Industry Designer of the Year award in 1984, having set up her company only five years before. She was known for her workwear-derived designs. But 1984, the year the slogan T-shirt went mainstream, marked a pinnacle in her career.

Designer Katherine Hamnett makes her antinuclear point as she meets Prime Minister Margaret Thatcher in 1984.

KATHARINE HEPBURN

fashion icon • born 1907

"View with Alarm the Strange Spectacle of Women in Trousers" ran the headline in an early 1930s newspaper article. It went on: "Many an intelligent girl rebels against this idea of developing her life to please men, so she makes a brave outward bid for equality by trying to act like a man." By 1933 sailor pants and beach pajamas were touted as the next new thing, and by 1937 women could go out and buy their own pantsuit, if they dared.

Katharine Hepburn was one Hollywood star who helped to pioneer women's casual clothing. She preferred to wear comfortable sportswear offscreen, and as a result her particular form of chic looked effortless and, at the time, masculine. Rather than skirts, she preferred "slacks"—heavier, more tailored pants complete with masculine pockets and pleats. For comfort she opted for low heels, sweaters, and pants instead of high heels and skirts. The Hepburn style included pantsuits, kimono jackets, loose men's sweaters, army jackets, and even caps. And when her studio tried to ban her for turning up to work in jeans, she fought them to the hilt—it's said that she threatened to walk out, in just a pair of silk knickers.

The camera snapped Ms. Hepburn playing tennis in pants, white sneakers, a cardigan worn over a sweater, and hair swept back, or sitting cross-legged doing her knitting in wide trousers and a buttoned-up shirt. Where Marlene Dietrich had shocked with her take on men's formal dress, Hepburn appropriated the slightly more acceptable male casual look. She wore just a trace of makeup and refused to conform to the offscreen groomed glamor of her peers.

"Hepburn has the lean thighs and broad bladelike shoulders of a mythical huntress," enthused *Vogue*. Katharine Hepburn was blessed with the boyishly slim, tall frame of a catwalk model. As a child she was a tomboy, climbing trees and cutting off her hair. As an adult she was independent, determined, and a law unto herself, an image that she often translated into her screen persona: tomboy Jo March in *Little Women* and as a pilot in *Christopher Strong* (female aviators epitomized the independent, emancipated woman). Perhaps her most famous role was alongside Humphrey Bogart in *The African Queen*, in 1951. She went on to win four Oscars.

If anyone could get away with wearing the pants, it was Hepburn.

Katharine Hepburn in London, March 1952, relaxed and casual
In a "masculine" pantsuit.

HERMÈS

Kelly bag • 1955

It was the stuff of fairytales. Movie star legend gets her prince and marries him. During her engagement to Prince Rainier of Monaco, the classy, well-groomed blonde Grace Kelly was often photographed carrying a certain Hermès bag—"the small tall bag with straps."

While the press went mad about the love match, French company Hermès enjoyed the free publicity and celebrity endorsement. The public had already nicknamed the bag "the Hermès." But as a tribute to the new princess, Hermès made a canny move and renamed it the "Kelly Bag" in 1955 to mark the royal wedding. The pair married in Monaco Cathedral the following year, and the world watched.

Naturally, Hermès was flooded with orders from copycats wanting a piece of Princess Grace's elegant style. After her marriage, the Kelly bag hit the headlines again, when the princess was rumored to have used her bag to hide her pregnancy from the prying eyes of the paparazzi. The Kelly bag quickly became the Hermès best-seller, and still remains the company's most popular bag today.

> *Hermès was flooded with orders from copycats wanting a piece of Princess Grace's elegant style. The Kelly bag quickly became the Hermès bestseller.*

Hermès was founded in 1837 as a harness maker and saddler—in fact, the Kelly bag was originally conceived as a saddlebag. A smaller version, the style that Grace Kelly took up, followed in 1935. The wedge-shaped geometric bag had a small handle and fastened at the front. Its saddle stitching, padlock, and distinctive Hermès-Paris insignia marked it out as an original. Kelly bags were painstakingly made by hand. Each one took 18 hours of hard labor, and demanded about 2,600 hand stitches.

Hermès wasn't to know that Princess Grace would not live happily ever after. But her tragic death in a car accident in 1982 only served to immortalize Kelly as the glamorous star of films *Rear Window* and *High Society*, wife of a prince, and namesake of a Hermès bag.

Prince Rainier and Princess Grace of Monaco in the 1950s. The princess carries her trademark Hermès bag.

DONNA KARAN

women's business suit • 1985

The power suit, with its wide shoulders and buttock-hugging skirt, became a symbol of the 1980s. Yet, in practical terms, it had flaws. Although many male designers made impeccably cut suits, they failed when it came to comfort and ease. Their power suits couldn't work for both day and evening, and were not ideal when it came to airplane seats or sneaked power naps.

American designer Donna Karan took a slightly different approach when she launched her own collection in 1985 with husband Stephan Weiss. She thought about the hectic lifestyles of New York working women running families and dominating boardrooms. And she asked herself: What clothes do I need and what do I like to wear?

She came up with a collection of simple, comfortable, and practical clothes. The Karan style was interchangeable smart but sexy separates in luxurious cashmere, wool, jersey, and stretch fabrics. The basic palette was black, white, and neutrals, with an optional flash of bright color.

"Men designing for women are designing for a fantasy—how they want a woman to look. They aren't living with their clothing as women designers are."

Karan's idea was that women could jump out of bed and first slip on a "body" as a foundation. These "bodies" were all-in-one basic garments, inspired by dancer Martha Graham's leotard. They looked similar to a swimsuit but fastened between the legs. Some had an attached shirt top, which would never come untucked. Karan did "bodies" in cashmere, jersey, and cotton. Then it was just a case of adding layers. The Karan business suit was a wraparound sarong skirt and a stretch blazer worn over a "body." Take off the blazer, and you instantly have a feminine skirt and top for the evening. And for warmth just throw on a cashmere wrap.

As a U.S. size 10 herself, Karan understood the importance of flattering the ordinary figure. At last, a woman was designing sympathetically for women. She explained in an interview: "Men designing for women are designing for a fantasy—how they want a woman to look. They aren't living with their clothing as women designers are."

A classic women's suit by Donna Karan. Smart yet comfortable, her suits offered women a whole new way of dressing.

KENZO

printed dress • 1970s

One of seven children, Japanese designer Kenzo Takada grew up in his father's tea house, surrounded by glamorous geishas, and watching traditional flower arranging and tea ceremonies. When he arrived in Paris for the first time in 1964, his sea voyage from Japan had introduced him to Egypt, Vietnam, Italy, and Hong Kong. The essence of Kenzo's style was underpinned by his Japanese roots, but his collections were like a whirlwind trip around the world. Kenzo returned again and again to inspiration gleaned from his travels.

Together with Issey Miyake, Kenzo became one of the first Japanese designers to influence international fashion. Yohji Yamamoto and Rei Kawakubo of Comme des Garçons were to follow. In 1970 he opened Jungle Jap, his first Paris shop. He rejected the glove-slim fitted shifts of the 1960s for voluminous dresses that freed the body, but were cut flat and wide like kimonos. Kenzo festooned his dresses with stripes and garlands of flowers. He used bold, bright colors and lively patterns. The press dubbed his new short, printed cotton shifts "the flower dresses."

Kenzo captured the hippie-trail spirit of the 1970s with his flamboyant East-meets-West style, raising the globetrotting look to high fashion.

Kenzo's oversized, carefree printed dresses are a symbol of the 1970s. Freedom, unconstricting shapes, and hanging loose appealed to the flower power generation. He came to Paris just at the time when women craved fluidity and print, and his designs were like a breath of fresh air. Kenzo layered exuberant floral prints of roses and peonies with patchwork, stripes, and pleats. He borrowed from folk traditions around the globe, making whirling Czechoslovakian and Romanian peasant smocks with layered striped skirts and elegant African-inspired toga dresses. In 1979 Kenzo took humble cotton jersey (T-shirt fabric) to new heights with his series of sophisticated striped summer dresses.

Kenzo captured the hippie-trail spirit of the 1970s with his flamboyant East-meets-West style, raising the globetrotting look to high fashion. And he gave a bra-burning generation the chance to let it all hang out.

Kenzo's autumn/winter collection for 1987/88, revealing the designer's characteristic passion for bright colors and bold prints.

GAP
KHAKIS

KHAKIS

fashion classic • 1940s–2000

The all-American smart-casual look, the dress-down Friday essential, is a pair of close-weave or cotton twill khaki pants, also known as chinos. They can be worn with a jacket, a T-shirt, or an open-necked shirt. Khakis have never had the bad-boy rebellious overtones of jeans. And it is generally accepted that Gap makes the best khakis.

The military began to use the dust-colored durable khaki twill for the uniforms of troops serving in hot countries. Greta Garbo, Marlene Dietrich, and Katharine Hepburn endorsed unisex khaki slacks as the new casual cool during the 1940s. And American ex-soldiers enrolling in college after World War II refused to give up their comfortable military chinos. The beige twill pants replaced dungarees and flannel trousers as the perfect campus uniform. Khakis were the chosen pants of Jack Kerouac's Beat Generation for a consciously sloppy style, worn with T-shirts and leather jackets. American adolescents took up the look.

Real estate developer Don Fisher started his shop Gap in California in 1969, selling Levi's jeans and records to the flower power generation. By the 1980s, Gap had expanded, offering chinos, T-shirts, and rails of wardrobe basics, and had dropped everything except its own-brand merchandise. The baby boomers, now frankly a little too old for jeans, took up khaki chinos and a shirt as their respectable offduty uniform.

Gap used clever marketing in order to promote chinos as a modern classic. The 1993 "Who wore khakis?" campaign showed old photographs of popular stars including Miles Davis, Pablo Picasso, James Dean, and Marilyn Monroe wearing their own khaki chinos. It tugged on the heart strings of those nostalgic for old-school glamor, and wove khakis into history. This sense of heritage managed to make the very ordinary pants seem highly desirable.

Gap is the great leveler—Americans young and old, rich and poor, all wear Gap. And Gap khakis now have their place in the roll call of ultimate casual basics.

Miles Davis wearing khakis, an image used by Gap in the
successful advertising campaign of 1993.

Bronzed models in brilliant white smalls—Calvin Klein is a master at creating attention-grabbing images.

CALVIN KLEIN

underwear • 1980s

Fashion designer or marketing genius? When it comes to Calvin Klein underwear, it has always been the slick marketing campaign that propels the product around the globe. In the early 1980s, Calvin Klein offered plain cotton underwear with a designer price tag to the masses—and they took the bait. And he put the sex back into smalls with his advertising campaigns. Up until 1983, men's underwear advertising had been fairly staid. Klein changed all that with startlingly titillating images.

He began with men's underwear—basic briefs and shorts with an elasticized band around the top bearing his name, and three styles of vest. But then he spent a reputed $500,000 on advertising. Photographer Bruce Weber's 1983 erotic photographs of the Olympic pole-vaulter Tom Hintinaus stopped traffic. Imagine a well-endowed man, shot from below, clad only in revealing cotton briefs. Klein hung the image on a giant billboard over Times Square. Hintinaus looked like a Greek god against the blue sky. When the ad appeared in bus shelters, vandals smashed the glass and stole every poster. Clever Klein had done it. Men—and the women who bought men's underwear for them—wanted his undies. So what if they were expensive?

Klein's next move was with gender-bender underwear for women, straight out of the men's locker room. In 1984 he gave girls plain boxer shorts complete with a buttoned fly-front, and a female version of the jockstrap with a wide logoed waistband. This campaign featured a female model in tight briefs and a T-shirt pulled right up, and almost off. The ultimate 1980s physique was gym-toned and strong for both men and women. Klein's sporty undies emphasized that androgynous super-body ideal. At a time when the underwear market pushed lacy, sexy designs on women, Klein gave them sport-sexy basics. And they couldn't get enough of them. The demand for Klein's women's boxer shorts went into overdrive, and by Christmas the shops were out of stock and had to reorder.

Klein realized that an aspirational image plus a good basic product is a winning formula. And just to push the point home, his 1990s ads featuring nearly nude rap star Marky Mark with a topless Kate Moss reputedly upped his underwear sales by nearly a third. Calvin Klein proved what everybody really knew anyway—sex sells.

RALPH LAUREN

Stars and Stripes • 1996

Ralph Lauren sells concepts, not clothes. "Style, not fashion," is his great cry. The son of Russian-Jewish immigrants, he grew up in the Bronx in New York and started off selling ties, but built his fortune on peddling the Great American Dream. He reinforces and idealizes hearth, home, and national identity. As *Elle* magazine explained in 1994: "Lauren's genius has been in giving women the kind of clothes which they associate with the best of their culture. Repackaging, adapting, inventing."

What could be more American than a sweat shirt or sweater bearing the image of the Star-Spangled Banner, or a cropped T-shirt with USA sprawled over the bust? Lauren's Stars and Stripes sweat shirts could be worn on the street, on the pitch, and at the gym. Lauren had grown up playing basketball and baseball, games that require comfortable, sporty clothes. But he also realized the link between status dressing and sportswear. The Stars and Stripes became an emblem associated with Ralph Lauren's clothes (as well as with Tommy Hilfiger's), so wearing a flag sweat shirt meant designer credibility to those in the know, silently proclaiming "I'm fashionable and rich enough to be wearing clothes by Ralph Lauren."

It was the launch of Lauren's Polo Jeans collection in 1996 that really put his adoption of the U.S. flag on the map. He plastered it over his merchandise, and sometimes, instead of the stars, had the nerve to put the letters "RL" in the top left-hand corner, so branding his own initials on the ultimate American symbol. It was clever and manipulative—but it worked. Male super-model Tyson posed for Polo Jeans in front of a huge U.S. flag painted with beige and red stripes (a homage to artist Jasper Johns).

And the symbol keeps on selling. In the weeks and months after the September 11 disaster, Americans, rallying against terrorism, reached into the mothballs and the bottom of their closets and dug out their old Lauren flag-emblem clothes.

Nowadays, true American classic clothes are still for sale for those moved to proclaim their patriotism. One of Lauren's popular sellers is a simple cotton/polyester sweat shirt, bearing the words "Polo USA" and a picture of the American flag.

Ralph Lauren's use of the Stars and Stripes revealed a huge talent
for tapping in to American patriotism and nostalgia.

Ralph Lauren

RALPH LAUREN

cowboy chic • 1978

At the beginning of the 1970s, designer Ralph Lauren, born Ralph Lipschitz in New York, in 1939, delved deep into the American psyche and came up with a rough and rugged Wild West style. He wanted to launch the romantic notion of cowboy Americana, marketing men's denim and chamois jeans to a nation hungry for frontier nostalgia. This cowboy range, cheaper than Lauren's mainline Polo collection, was named Chaps. And on the Chaps letterhead was a picture of a rider galloping past a group of cheering goldminers. Even then, Lauren knew he would be in the money.

During the 1970s, Lauren won acclaim for many of his collections, as well as for his designs for hit movies like *The Great Gatsby* and Woody Allen's *Annie Hall*. But it was some years on, in 1978, that he hit the jackpot with the cowboy look, this time with a collection named Western for his Ralph Lauren women's wear line. His cowgirls came whooping and shooting down the runway. They wore satin cowboy shirts, suede-fringed leather jackets, shearling coats, prairie skirts, vests with racoon-tail fringes, and silver cowboy belt buckles, and all to the soundtrack of "Back in the Saddle Again." The fashionable public loved his hip-shootin', freewheeling style.

> *His cowgirls ... wore satin cowboy shirts, suede-fringed leather jackets, shearling coats, prairie skirts, vests with racoon-tail fringes, and silver cowboy belt buckles.*

And to cash in on the trend at high-street level, Lauren teamed up with popular chain store Gap for a subsidiary label, offering cheap corduroy jeans, leather ties, lizard belts, and corduroy coats. The Wild West look was in. But it was short lived. By 1980, the cowboy theme was dead and buried.

Like Calvin Klein, Lauren is a marketing genius. "The dreams sell the clothes," he admitted in a 1993 *Women's Wear Daily* interview. He accepted his 1987 Retailer of the Year award wearing jeans, cowboy boots, and a black dinner jacket (and was duly criticized for it). And he even posed for his own 1987 ad campaign in a stetson and cowboy boots on a ranch in California. Lauren lives and trades on his own glamorized version of the American Dream.

A Ralph Lauren ad from the 1970s, showing the all-American frontier checks that typified his cowboy and prairie looks.

LEATHER JACKET

fashion classic • 1950s–1980s

From the 1950s to the 1980s, the black leather jacket spelled danger to concerned parents of impressionable teenagers. It was the uniform for thugs and bad boys. It conjured up every mother's worst nightmare—S&M, gangs fighting in the streets, gay cruisers in peaked caps, heroin-addled punks, tattooed Hell's Angels, heavy metallers, and even Nazi soldiers. And this is why, for 30 years, young men and women saved up for their leathers. The black leather jacket was a sartorial signal that said "I belong" to whichever leather-jacketed youth tribe they aspired to. And it screamed "I'm rebelling" at the older generation.

So where did it all start? During World War I, German pilots wore leather jackets. Then Americans took them up as industrial workwear. In World War II, both sides wore leathers—SS soldiers, bomber pilots, and submarine crews. In postwar America, the police adopted the black leather jacket, as did frustrated ex-soldiers unable to sink back into civilian life. These bikers roamed around on motorbikes and quickly became associated with drinking, brawling, and unruly bike racing. When thousands of these outlaws on wheels descended on small Californian towns, Stanley Kramer decided to make a film about it. *The Wild One* (1954) starred a swaggering Marlon Brando and a black leather-clad biker gang. With Brando's endorsement, the leather jacket became the height of rebel cool, and teenage bad boys saved up to buy a square-cut "Perfecto" or "Bronx" jacket just like his.

The baton passed to the British-based Rockers in the 1960s. They wore black leather with dirty jeans on big bikes—the ultimate contrast to their rivals, the Mods, with their tailored Italianate suits and scooters. The Rockers painted and patched their leathers and added studs and chains.

In the late 1970s, punk reared its spitting, cursing head. These anarchists (their mantra was "No Future") went to battle with the establishment. And leather jackets spattered with spiked metal studs, daubed with slogans, and covered with badges, zippers, and chains were part of their nihilist uniform.

But by the 1980s, the shock factor of the black leather jacket was diminished. Designers put them on the catwalk, the high street copied, and they hit the mainstream.

First worn by servicemen in World War I, the black leather jacket—here the
classic square-cut Perfecto—became a lasting symbol of rebellion.

SUZANNE LENGLEN

fashion icon • 1899–1938

French tennis star Suzanne Lenglen first entertained Wimbledon audiences with her athletic on-court leaps and bounds when she just 15 years old. She also shocked them with her racy, flapper-style rolled-down stockings, held up with garters rather than suspenders.

The glamorous, athletic Lenglen, who won every Wimbledon women's final from 1919 to 1926, changed attitudes toward what women should wear on court. She rejected the expected long skirt, sedate shirt, and tie, and instead opted for a loose, thin, sleeveless dress, or a sweater and skirt that only just reached below the knee. And she wore these, it was scandalously rumored, without petticoats or corsets.

Lenglen had called upon French designer Jean Patou to design her on-court and off-court wardrobe. Patou was a purist. His daywear borrowed from sportswear designs, with no-frills simplicity, comfort, and ease. And he also specialized in specific sports clothing for swimming, riding, and skiing. When Lenglen played in his sleeveless cardigans, pleated silk skirts, and bright orange headbands, the look set a fashion trend both on court and off.

Along with his contemporary, Coco Chanel, Patou helped to redefine women's dress during the 1920s. He made clothes for the slim, fit bodies of the *garçonnes* age (the term came from the censored French novel *La Garçonne*, about the antics of sexually liberated, short-haired career women). Thanks to Patou, Lenglen came to be an icon of the 1920s. Fitness and athleticism became a symbol of modernity and youth, and influenced the way women dressed. Suntans were in. Fresh air was encouraged. And, of course, women now needed the exercise to get the figure to fit the clothes.

Russian impresario Sergei Diaghilev and French writer and director Jean Cocteau immortalized Ms Lenglen and her sportswear in their 1924 Ballet Russes production, *Le Train Bleu*. Lenglen inspired the leading role, the Tennis Player. Chanel, as costume designer, dressed Nijinska in white from head to toe—opaque stockings, a loose, silky tennis dress, and matching headband. *Le Train Bleu*, with its bathers, golf players, and athletic dancers, and its curtain painted by Pablo Picasso, summed up the sports mania of the 1920s.

Tennis star and fashion icon Suzanne Lenglen lunges for a shot at Wimbledon, July 1922.

LEVI'S 501s

fashion classic • 1890s

When a customer complained to Nevada tailor Jacob Davis that his pockets were giving way, Davis introduced metal rivets to strengthen the seams. His new pants proved so popular that he decided to patent the idea. He approached Levi Strauss, a Bavarian bedding, clothing, and underwear wholesaler in San Francisco, then a gold rush town. In 1873 Davis and Strauss began to make tough workmen's pants, then called "waist overalls." They used strong indigo cotton denim from a New Hampshire mill, with copper rivets to strengthen the pockets and the base of the fly. Denim, or *serge de Nîmes*, was originally imported from France, but Americans started manufacturing their own in the eighteenth century.

The gold miners and laborers of the West couldn't get enough of the tough pants, which were strong enough to hold pocketfuls of gold. A numbering system helped retailers order for their stores, and in the 1890s, Davis and Strauss's best-quality denim pants were assigned lot number 501. Blue jeans became the workwear of ranchers, cowboys, lumberjacks, and farmers, and by the 1920s, 501s were the market leaders. In 1936 the distinctive red tab was added—now 501 originals would stand out from the copies.

It was only in the 1950s that, spurred on by film icons such as James Dean, U.S. teenage rebels began to regard jeans as fashionable, and Europe started to import them. Europe's teenagers wanted a share of American postwar prosperity, and rock 'n' rolling in Levi's 501s gave them exactly that.

In the 1980s, 501s became a unisex street uniform. An advertising campaign featuring a model stripping off his 501s in a laundromat helped to fuel sales. The kids of the 1980s wanted their jeans ripped and torn—ironic, as rivets to prevent rips and tears were the original concept behind the 501.

Levi's 501s are the oldest, and still the bestselling, jeans by Levi Strauss & Co. They have been in demand for over a century and still remain a classic. Today, the company makes 501 jeans in more than 100 sizes, and 20 fabrics and finishes. The 501 is an all-time favorite.

The jeans that clothed the world: classic Levi's 501s, a best-seller for well over a hundred years.

*Canny Coco Chanel made the little black dress an essential part of
every woman's wardrobe.*

THE LITTLE BLACK DRESS

fashion classic • 1926

Who else but the unstoppable Coco Chanel could raise the simple black dress to high fashion? Before the 1920s, a black dress was associated with those in mourning, those in service, or those too poor to afford pale colors that showed the dirt. Chanel had the nerve to run against the tide of convention. Her black crèpe de Chine sheath dress of 1926, with its short skirt and long sleeves, redefined women's fashion. It was revolutionary both for its color and its unadorned boyish cut. American *Vogue* hailed it as a classic, a uniform, comparing it to the black Ford Model T car.

Chanel took the grief out of black. Postwar black dresses were a common sight. Many young women mourned their men—Chanel herself lost her lover, Boy Capel, in 1919. Black as widows' weeds conveyed a social subtext: womanhood not girlhood, experience, independence, and sophistication.

So Chanel's new invention could be daringly sexy and sophisticated, particularly when worn by unmarried women. With clean lines borrowed from men's clothes, it conveyed power and self-sufficiency. On both sides of the Atlantic women had sipped the nectar of equality during the war, and the simple black dress hinted that women could go it alone without their men—widows or not—and still look glamorous.

A little black dress was practical and economical. It didn't show the dirt, and it flattered and slimmed the figure. It served as a blank canvas to emphasize elaborate jewelry, a pretty face, or blonde hair. It had chameleon qualities: A clever woman could dress the same piece up with costume jewelry for evening or keep it plain for day. A black dress could be glamorous in velvet or lace, or simple in wool. And both shop girls and heiresses could afford to wear one, albeit not by Chanel.

Once women tried the little black dress, there was no going back. Chanel had created a blueprint for future generations, and the little black dress would endure the test of time.

ALEXANDER McQUEEN

Highland Rape collection • 1995

To present a womenswear collection called Highland Rape, or even use the word "rape" in conjunction with fashion, was just plain cheeky. Asking for trouble. British designer and cab driver's son Alexander McQueen, about whom there were already whispers of misogyny, didn't care. In fact, his autumn/winter 1995 show, just two years after his London Fashion Week debut, was not about raped women—it was about England's rape of Scotland, the Jacobite rebellion, and the horrors of the Clearances. The *Evening Standard* reported: "The politically correct police were frozen like rabbits caught in the car headlamps.... The models appeared wild and distraught, some theatrically staggering, others driven down the blasted, thistle-strewn catwalk as if possessed by demons." It was a definitive moment in McQueen's career. It got him press coverage, controversy—and praise for his clothes.

The styling was risqué, blood-spattered, and wild. But the clothes were great: razor sharp military jackets, wide-legged pants, and one-sleeved jackets. Fabrics included second-skin rubbers, ripped suede, slashed and torn lace, boiled wool treated to look like moss, and tailored plaid. And McQueen used clever cutting to reveal erotic slices of skin. It was his expert tailoring that held the collection together.

The styling was risqué, blood-spattered, and wild. But the clothes were great: razor-sharp military jackets, wide-legged pants, and one-sleeved jackets.

The Highland Rape collection is typical of McQueen, the provocative East End genius who has worked both in a pie and mash shop and on Savile Row. He said in *i-D* magazine in 1997: "If I've influenced fashion it's by pissing everyone off." He is still criticized as a misogynist—a *Daily Mail* McQueen article in 2001 was entitled "The Designer Who Hates Women"—but he is recognized for his talent. The industry named him British Designer of the Year in 1996 and 2001, and he received the award jointly with John Galliano in 1997.

In 1996 McQueen went on to head up the design team at the Paris house of Givenchy. He is now a key player in the top echelons of international fashion.

Alexander McQueen's controversial Highland Rape collection hits the catwalk, autumn/winter 1995.

MADONNA

fashion icon • born 1958

Popstar Madonna's sexy, slutty, New York street style put the fear into parents, and drew impressionable teenage girls to her like a magnet. She wore lacy tights under ripped jeans, leggings under miniskirts, layered cropped tops, fingerless gloves, and fishnet skirts. She unashamedly flaunted her lace bras, and she topped her look with a mop of unruly streaked blonde hair. Madonna paid homage to punk with studded belts and scores of rubber bracelets on her arms. And she shocked her fellow Catholics with dangling crucifix earrings and by blasphemously stringing rosaries around her neck. In 1984 she had the nerve to release a song sweetly entitled "Like a Virgin."

Thanks to Madonna, the American bra business boomed. Women wanted lacy, sexy underwear, rubber "Virgin" bracelets, and anything with a cross on it. For the lead role in the 1985 film, *Desperately Seeking Susan*, she dressed as she did in real life. Copycat fans flocked to her concerts in fishnets and lace, weighed down with crucifixes and beads.

This trashy, provocative style was Madonna's first flirtation with the power of image. She learned very quickly how to use her personal style to seduce and manipulate the public. Her sexy image was a form of power. Many found this distinctly unnerving. British journalist Julie Burchill compared her to a woman who "looks like a slut and thinks like a man." But Madonna moved fast, always staying one step ahead of her fans. Just when you thought that Madonna had gone too far, she would reemerge in demure 1940s dresses or in full 1930s filmstar regalia.

This trashy, provocative style was Madonna's first flirtation with the power of image. She learned very quickly how to use her style to seduce and manipulate the public.

Madonna's carefully controlled image has helped her to remain a pop idol for 20 years. "Strike a pose, There's nothing to it," she commanded in her hit single "Vogue"—and her own poses have ranged from raven-haired, red-lipped geisha girl to demure, Chloé-clad wife and mother. She was never destined to be a one-hit wonder.

Madonna's trashy, punky look in Desperately Seeking Susan, *1985, just one of her many influential styles over two decades.*

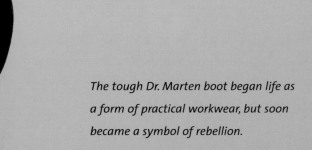

The tough Dr. Marten boot began life as a form of practical workwear, but soon became a symbol of rebellion.

KLAUS MARTEANS

Dr. Marten boots • 1950s–2000

Renowned as the macho footwear of skinheads, punks, and violent soccer hooligans, the Dr. Marten boot was actually first conceived to heal injury rather than cause it. When 25-year-old frontline soldier Dr. Klaus Marteans broke his foot skiing in the Bavarian Alps, he came up with a plan. Take a traditional army boot, but exchange the uncomfortable hard leather sole for an air-filled version to cushion the foot.

After World War II, Marteans teamed up with a mechanical engineer, Dr. Herbert Funck, and went into business in Munich, Germany. For soles, they bought old rubber dirt cheap from former Luftwaffe airfields; for eyelets they used the regimental numbers from old army jackets; and for uppers they cut up the leather pants of ex-army officers. Surprisingly, their best clients during the 1950s were older women, who appreciated the comfort of the boots. In 1960 Griggs Company imported Dr. Martens to Britain, adding distinctive yellow stitching. Soon factory workers, mailmen, and construction workers were walking on air.

To British youth subculture, the Dr. Marten boot made an antifashion working-class statement. It became part of a tribal uniform. When the police banned the skinheads' steel-capped army boots, they turned to Dr. Martens, which they wore sizes too big, for effect. In the 1970s, soccer hooligans painted their DMs with team colors. The customized Dr. Marten boot quickly became the punk footwear of choice. British bands the Clash and Madness wore them, and singer Ian Dury immortalized them in his album *New Boots and Panties*. Ironically, in the same decade, the Dr. Marten became part of the British police's official uniform. The soft soles meant they could stalk and surprise criminals, while the high boots were perfect for protecting the shins.

When Japanese designers Rei Kawakubo of Comme des Garçons and Yohji Yamamoto pillaged street fashion and raised Doc Martens to catwalk level, they set a trend, which then filtered back down to the high street. In the 1980s, Doc Martens became part of the mainstream street uniform of the fashionable—and this time there were no anti-establishment connotations.

Since its inception, the Doc Marten boot has infiltrated nearly every corner of society. In 1990 readers of music paper the *NME* voted Dr. Martens Fashion Item of the Year, the ultimate tribute to their favorite boot.

NOLAN MILLER

costumes for *Dynasty* • 1980s

Big shoulders. Big hair. Big cleavages. The women of *Dynasty*'s high-rolling Carrington and Colby families swept across the world's TV screens in their sequins and power suits—bitch-fighting, scheming, and seducing. "The women would be extraordinarily beautiful and they would wear the prettiest clothing imaginable. But they would not be window-dressing ... They would engage men competitively in business and with equal passion in bed," wrote Esther Shapiro, co-creator of the series, in the book *Dynasty, The Authorized Biography of the Carringtons*. It was the 1980s, and designer Nolan Miller's costumes for the soap opera epito-mized the decade where money talked, vulgarity ruled, and demure became a dirty word. His studio worked at record speed, rolling out more than 25 outfits each week.

Miller gave audiences glamor to dream of—fluid draped jersey dresses, fur wraps, puffed sleeves, killer suits, and dresses dripping with diamanté, beading, and lamé.

"All the other actresses wore simple silk shirts and gabardine trousers or skirts. I thought that was boring, so when I came on the scene, I persuaded the designer Nolan Miller to let me wear haute couture clothes with padded shoulders," wrote Joan Collins—*Dynasty*'s glamor queen super-bitch Alexis Colby—about the show in her book, *My Secrets*. "Then everyone suddenly wanted to become chic, so Nolan had to make me more outrageous than the others to fit in with my character. My shoulder pads got bigger and bigger—my hats more bizarre, my heels higher, my skirts shorter: it became ridiculous."

Texan-born Miller had arrived in Hollywood with dreams of becoming the next Adrian or Travis Banton, the legendary film costume designers of the 1930s. Although Miller had to make do with television, he still managed to give audiences glamor to dream of—fluid draped jersey dresses, fur wraps, puffed sleeves, killer suits, and dresses dripping with diamanté, beading, and lamé. And he put shoulder pads on everything, from silk shirts to fantasy frocks to night-dresses, harking back to the glamorous style of Adrian and Banton. Endorsed by the soap stars, larger-than-life characters, big shoulders began to be associated with power—and power dressing in the 1980s was big business.

Dressed to kill: Dynasty's Krystle Carrington and Alexis Colby do
battle in the big hair and glam stakes, dressed by Nolan Miller.

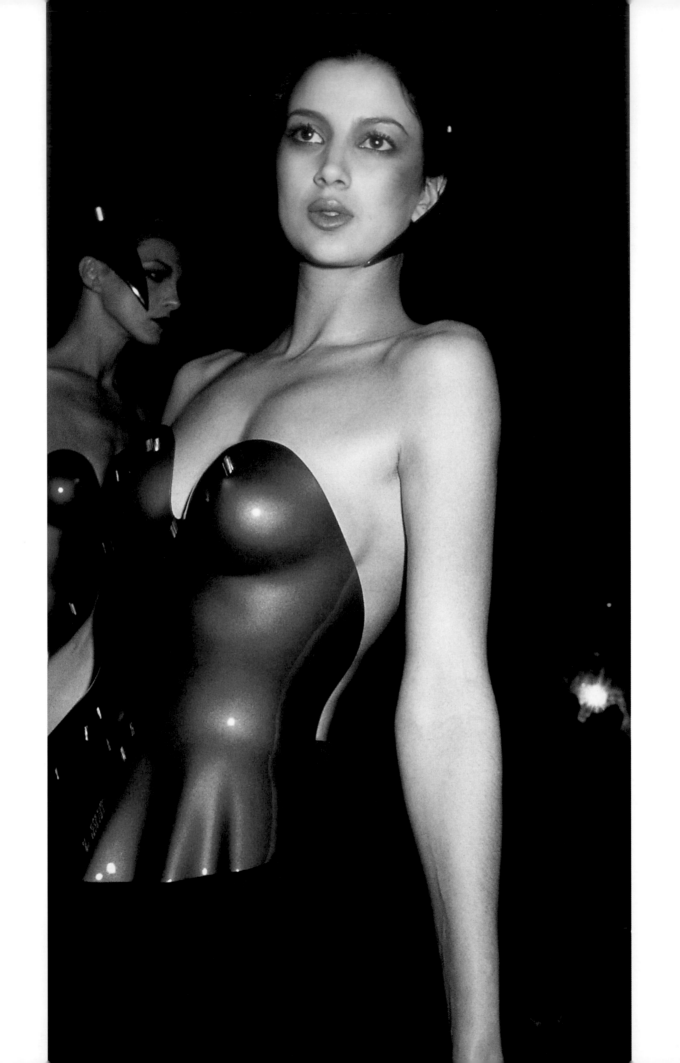

ISSEY MIYAKE

molded body corset • 1980s

Issey Miyake is a genius, a visionary, and a master of invention. He started showing his collections in Paris in 1973, and from then on went where no other fashion designer dared to tread.

Miyake's childhood was not solely a charmed one of geishas, falling cherry blossom, and tea houses. He was supposedly bicycling to school on August 6, 1945, when a bomb dropped on his hometown—Hiroshima. He had to deal with death, brutality, and regeneration. And he had experienced modern invention as a force of destruction.

It is not surprising that Miyake's pieces such as his rigid body corset seem like protective body armor, fending off attack. He is a designer with a postapocalyptic vision. But rather than looking back, his work is filled with optimism and hope for the future. Mark Holborn writes in his book *Issey Miyake*: "As much at home in the third Millennium as in Japanese tradition, he designs for the golden mean—clothes to dress a samurai or a bladerunner."

"Clothing is just an extension of our bodies and skin," explained Miyake in the *Sunday Times* in 1992. His plastic molded bustier, designed at the beginning of the 1980s, explores just this idea. It looks like a naked woman's torso, complete with tummy button, nipples, and curvaceous stomach flesh. On the one hand, it mimics the vulnerability of naked skin; on the other, it offers hard protection for the soft belly that will lie underneath. It is like impenetrable, voluptuous, strap-on skin—natural in its form, but artificial in its shiny, high-tech red plastic.

Miyake's designs are like moving, walking, living sculptures. He has no qualms about taking rigid industrial materials like plastic and using them in place of fabric. He designed one bustier out of coils of wire, for example, and used wicker to construct a cagelike black and red top. Whether in pleated fabric or molded plastic, Miyake's designs often stand away from the body, just as a Japanese kimono allows space between the fabric and the flesh.

The molded body corset is an example of Miyake at his best—blurring the boundaries between sculpture and fashion, and using the human form to express his vision of the future.

A model shows off Issey Miyake's sculptural molded body corset,
which simultaneously reveals and protects the figure.

KATE MOSS

fashion icon • born 1974

When little Kate Moss arrived on the London fashion scene, she was like a breath of fresh air. She was no diva like her supermodel predecessors. She was only 5 feet 7 inches (1.7m). And she came from Croydon, a distinctly unglamorous suburb of London.

Moss offered what the supermodels lacked: girl-next-door accessibility. She was beautiful, but she was also ordinary. While the supers thundered down the runway, Moss was the small girl who held her own beside them. With her versatile good looks, she was like a blank canvas—she could be made to look innocent one day and sophisticated the next.

Moss was the Twiggy of the 1990s. Sarah Doukas of Storm model agency discovered her in 1988 at New York's JFK airport, as she returned from a family holiday. Corinne Day photographed her for *The Face* magazine, and from there she went on to become an international cover girl and the face of Calvin Klein, aged only 18. She modeled nude for Klein's Obsession campaign.

Moss symbolized the end of the diva era and ushered in a new trend for thin "waif" models who suited grunge dressing, the fashion trend of the moment. The press lambasted these models for encouraging eating disorders and glamorizing drug-taking, labeling it "heroin chic." And yes, Miss Moss did do time in rehab in the late 1990s, but, she claimed, for alcohol.

A conversation between photographer Mario Testino and Kate Moss appeared in *The Face* in 1999. "There's few girls that can last 11 years and still look beautiful and people are into them. Because people get bored of people. But they never get bored of you," he tells her. "There's an innocence always—whatever you do, you carry on looking like an innocent girl. And people don't get bored of innocence."

A girl with attitude, Kate Moss is not just a pretty face. With her highly individual way of dressing off the catwalk, she has become a style icon.

Kate Moss models Versace haute couture, 1993. The skinny girl-next-door became the face of the 1990s.

Nike's Air Jordan trainers, created in 1984. Classic designs like these
are as sought-after as later, more extreme sneaker styles.

NIKE

Air Jordan • 1984

Michael J. Jordan of the Chicago Bulls was a basketball legend, rated one of the game's greatest ever players. In 1984 Jordan became captain of the US basketball team that won a gold at the Los Angeles Olympics. He was named National Basketball Association (NBA) Rookie of the Year. That same year, he collaborated with Nike's Tinker Hatfield, and together they came up with the Air Jordan basketball shoe. It was one of the most high-profile celebrity endorsements in sport history—rumor had it that Jordan was paid millions of dollars for the pleasure.

The first Air Jordan trainers had leather uppers in the red, black, and white Chicago Bulls team colors. The herringbone pattern on the sole was devised to help the player move quickly in any direction. The air-cushioned heels gave bounce and comfort, and the high ankle design supported the foot. But the NBA fined Jordan $5,000 for flouting basketball rules and wearing shoes with more than two colors on court. They were banned three days later. This only served to quicken Air Jordans' elevation to cult status.

The Air Jordan became a collector's piece. As sneaker chic spread, Air Jordans became a fashion statement, not just a shoe for basketball enthusiasts.

Spike Lee starred as a Michael Jordan-worshiping character, Mars Blackmon, in his 1986 film *She's Gotta Have It*. And in 1988 Nike produced an Air Jordan ad campaign, with Spike (as Mars) appearing on court with Jordan. On new editions of the sneaker, Nike replaced its "swoosh" insignia with Jordan's "jumpman" logo.

The Air Jordan became a collector's piece. As sneaker chic spread, Air Jordans became a fashion statement, not just a shoe for basketball enthusiasts. This was, after all, at the height of mid-1980s sneaker mania, when traditional sports clothing became fashionable as daywear.

But the flip side of the shoe's success was that Air Jordans became a major target of "sneaker-jacking," a humiliating—and occasionally highly violent—form of mugging that left the victim to walk home without any shoes.

TOMMY NUTTER

Savile Row suit • 1970s

Tommy Nutter, master tailor and black sheep of London's prestigious Savile Row, the home of bespoke tailoring, was the man who "put the haute into men's couture clothing," according to *Country Life* magazine in 1978. The ex-plumber's assistant and civil servant opened his tailoring business on St. Valentine's Day in 1969. He helped to pull Savile Row out of the dark ages and into the present, and was the first on the Row to open up the shop windows to the public. Somehow, he persuaded hip young Londoners to ditch their jeans, T-shirts, and flower power, and to wriggle into his Savile Row made-to-measure suits.

Other menswear designers offered cigarette-slim suits at the end of the 1960s. But Nutter broke with convention. "[He] established a style of his own, a style of the house clearly influenced by early Cardin," declared the *Times* in 1977. "Narrow, square, pagoda shoulders, with extravagantly broad lapels often widely braided, tight waists and tightly crotched but flared trousers." The overall effect was sharp, voluminous but sleek. Nutter put the sex back into made-to-measure suits. They looked good and they were underpinned by Savile Row-standard tailoring. Tommy Nutter, a trained architect, was a master of clothing construction.

Somehow, Nutter persuaded hip young Londoners to ditch their jeans, T-shirts, and flower power, and to wriggle into his Savile Row made-to-measure suits.

The in-crowd flocked to Nutter for their suits—the Beatles, Mick Jagger, and Ossie Clark. When Bianca Jagger stormed into the House of Nutter and demanded a suit just like Mick's, Tommy knew he was on to a good thing. Bianca cut off her waist-length hair to complement her new sharp but slouchy three-piece suit, and set it off with a dandy's walking cane. In 1969 in Gibraltar, Yoko Ono and John Lennon tied the knot in matching his and hers white suits by Tommy Nutter. Soon Joan Collins, Diana Rigg, Twiggy, and Barbra Streisand all wanted one too. Mr. Nutter was the toast of Savile Row.

In 1976 Nutter jumped ship and left the company he had created to work for Savile Row tailoring firm Kilgour French Stanbury.

Maverick tailor Tommy Nutter in his Savile Row shop, November 1969, wearing one of his own flamboyant checked suits.

JACKIE ONASSIS

fashion icon • 1929–1994

When she entered the White House in 1961, Jacqueline Kennedy was only 31 years old, the third youngest First Lady in history. And she was already a star in her own right. On the campaign trail, crowds doubled if Jackie showed up with her husband. She had youth and style, and injected American politics with a much-needed dose of glamor. She stood out from her predecessors and the retinue of badly dressed politicians' wives. And she knew it.

After being criticized for wearing Parisian fashion (Givenchy and Balenciaga were favorites), Jackie asked the aristocratic U.S.-based Oleg Cassini to design her working wardrobe. His fawn dress and matching coat for the presidential inauguration in 1961 were a success. Uncluttered coats worn over matching shiftdresses became an essential component of Jackie's uniform. The knee-length dresses emphasized her slim hips and elegant bearing. She wore them sleeveless in linen and silk, sometimes slashed with a boat neckline. The coats were fitted, or flared in the trapeze style, often with three-quarter-length sleeves. Cassini restricted detail to large covered buttons, tassels, or collar detailing. The fashion statement was clean lines and plain colors.

Jackie used fashion to woo her husband's public. She had exquisite good taste and an eye for discreet clothes that suited her. And with Diana Vreeland, who had stints as editor on American *Vogue* and *Harper's Bazaar*, as adviser, she never looked like a clothes horse. Typically clever Jackie tricks were to use color, to stand out in a crowd, and simplicity where others went over the top with furs and frills.

When she went to Paris in 1961, wearing Givenchy and Oleg Cassini, she was feted by the press, and proved the point that even America's women could look chic. Jackie the style icon was born. "The 'Jackie Look' was a regular selling-point on Seventh Avenue, where everything she was photographed wearing was translated into cheaper copies," wrote Sarah Bradford in *America's Queen: The Life of Jacqueline Kennedy Onassis*. Other women realized that the coat and shiftdress could be a working uniform for them too, and they adopted it.

Jackie redefined the role of First Lady as youthful and stylish. And she set an impossible precedent for the presidents' wives who followed in her wake.

Jacqueline Kennedy Onassis arrives in London, in 1970, wearing Yves Saint Laurent and her trademark dark glasses.

PAUL POIRET

harem pants • 1909

When producer Sergei Diaghilev's Ballets Russes came whirling into Paris in 1909, the opulent extravagance of Léon Bakst's exotic costumes stunned couturier Paul Poiret. In the ballet *Schéhérazade*, a blue-painted Nijinsky danced the Gold Slave wearing a pair of loose Turkish pants bound at the waist and gathered at the ankle. A wave of exoticism and Fauvist color filtered through Poiret's collections. He introduced turbans, feathered plumes, and kimonos. And his 1909 women's wear collection included his own version of the Turkish trousers, known as harem pants. Imagine long, wide, voluminous trousers, almost like divided skirts, pulled in at the ankle with a band of fabric.

The loosely draped construction of the harem pants was typical of Poiret. By designing clothes that used flowing fabric for maximum comfort and ease, he tried to liberate women from restrictive underwear and bustling petticoats.

Harem pants were not an instant success. It was not until the 1920s that women accepted harem pants and wide pajama trousers as evening wear—and even then, only the very fashionable and avant-garde chose pants instead of skirts. By then, women were beginning to take traditionally masculine clothing and make it their own. They chopped their hair into short Eton crops and smoked cigarettes. Yet it was still considered risqué for women to wear pants. British writer Evelyn Waugh wrote in *Vile Bodies*, his chronicle of 1920s high life: "It was a long and cold drive. Miss Runcible wore trousers and Miles touched up his eyelashes in the dining room of the hotel where they stopped for luncheon. So they were asked to leave."

By designing clothes that used flowing fabric for maximum comfort and ease, Poiret tried to liberate women from restrictive underwear and bustling petticoats.

By the 1930s, it might have still counted as bold for women to wear harem pants and pajamas, but it was no longer scandalous. Poiret's harem pants had helped to convince women that trousers were not only for men.

Only fashionable or daring women wore Paul Poiret's harem pants—but they showed that women could wear trousers, too.

MIUCCIA PRADA

Prada backpack and bag • 1990s

Prada bags were the status symbols of the 1990s. The fashion pack was hooked. "Kate Reardon of *Tatler* and Kim Stringer of *Elle* both have five; Jackie Modlinger, *Daily Express*, has 20," declared the *Evening Standard* in 1994. "Every fashion editor in town is itching to buy more but they can't get to the store in time ... Twice a year they all go to Milan for the shows. The second their Manolos hit the ground, it's on your marks, dump your bag at the hotel, and run like hell ... to the Prada shop. The sight, says one, resembles a little scuttling trail of ants."

It started with an all-black nylon backpack with no logo, launched in the mid-1980s by feminist, trained mime artist, and member of the Communist Party, Miuccia Prada. In 1978 she took over the ailing family business, which since 1913 had supplied luxury luggage to Italy's aristocracy. She treated nylon as carefully as her ancestors had treated leather. The black backpack, machine-made in a parachute factory, was practical and light. Inspired by sportswear and military backpacks, it was the ultimate in street-wise luxury; a breath of fresh air in a decade when design focused on loud logos and in-your-face excess. Miuccia Prada did finally add her own logo to her backpack, if only to identify it from the copies. But it was subtle—a flat, triangular metal tag.

> *Prada's formula was to identify with the needs of the modern woman, to introduce industrial materials to luxury luggage, and to keep her style understated.*

Miuccia Prada's winning formula was to identify with the needs of the modern woman, to introduce industrial materials to luxury luggage, and to keep her style understated. The high street copied her every move, and the fashionable parted with serious money for even simple designs, such as a PVC handbag, because they bore the Prada name. The range has included black nylon shoppers, nylon quilted bags, satin bags with Eastern leaf prints, bowling bags, silk bags with perspex handles, satchels with long shoulder straps, and many more.

Miuccia is the world's favorite bag lady, creating the handbags of dreams. The *Guardian* got it right in 1995 when it ran a headline including the words: "Happiness is a Prada bag."

Miuccia Prada is the queen of bags, creating desirable yet practical bags for both Prada and her diffusion line, Miu Miu.

MARY QUANT

miniskirt • 1965

If London was the epicenter of the Swinging Sixties, then Mary Quant was its queen. As a schoolgirl, she reworked her gingham uniform into short Bardot dresses. When, in 1958, she couldn't find the right clothes to fill her King's Road boutique, Bazaar, she bought fabric from Harrods and ran up a collection of pinafores and dresses on her sewing machine. She set a trend. And when her miniskirt hit the mainstream in 1965, it would become the symbol of an era.

Quant offered simple, childlike short skirts and pinafores in bright colors to women who didn't want to dress like their mothers. Her designs were young and classless and borrowed from the slick, tailored suits of the Mods. Quant dared the baby-boom generation to run free in pleated, high-waisted gymslips that served only to make the legs look longer. The fashionable silhouette now belonged to Twiggy rather than Marilyn Monroe. Hips and busts had had their day—the cool cats of the 1960s had discovered legs as the new erogenous zone. "All eyes are on legs: The longer, the leggier; the bolder, the better," explained Harper's Bazaar in 1967.

Mary Quant's mini was a sartorial statement that was about more than just fashion. It stood for a generation who had been sexually liberated by the contraceptive pill, who were to riot on the streets of Paris, who were opening their own boutiques, making their own music, and weren't ashamed to flaunt their legs. Youth called the shots, set the trends, and shocked its elders. The British government of Harold Wilson even funded research on the effect of the minidress. "We were showing knee-high cowboy boots worn with fantastically short skirts.... Eyebrows went right up to the hairline when the first model appeared. One girl carried an enormous shotgun; another swung a dead pheasant triumphantly around her head," says Quant of her first fashion show.

Coco Chanel denounced the mini as "disgusting," but nobody listened. Quant set up a wholesale operation, the Ginger Group, to mass-produce her designs. By 1966 Quant's miniskirts had reached a daring mid-thigh, and by 1969, the indecent micromini was only just skimming the buttocks. In 1966 Quant—described in 1962 Vogue as looking like "one of those child heroines"—received an OBE. When she heard the news, she apparently exclaimed: "I can hardly believe it ... but what's it going to be like curtseying in a miniskirt [to the Queen]?"

Mary Quant, modeling her trademark bob hairstyle, between two models in miniskirts, Milan 1967.

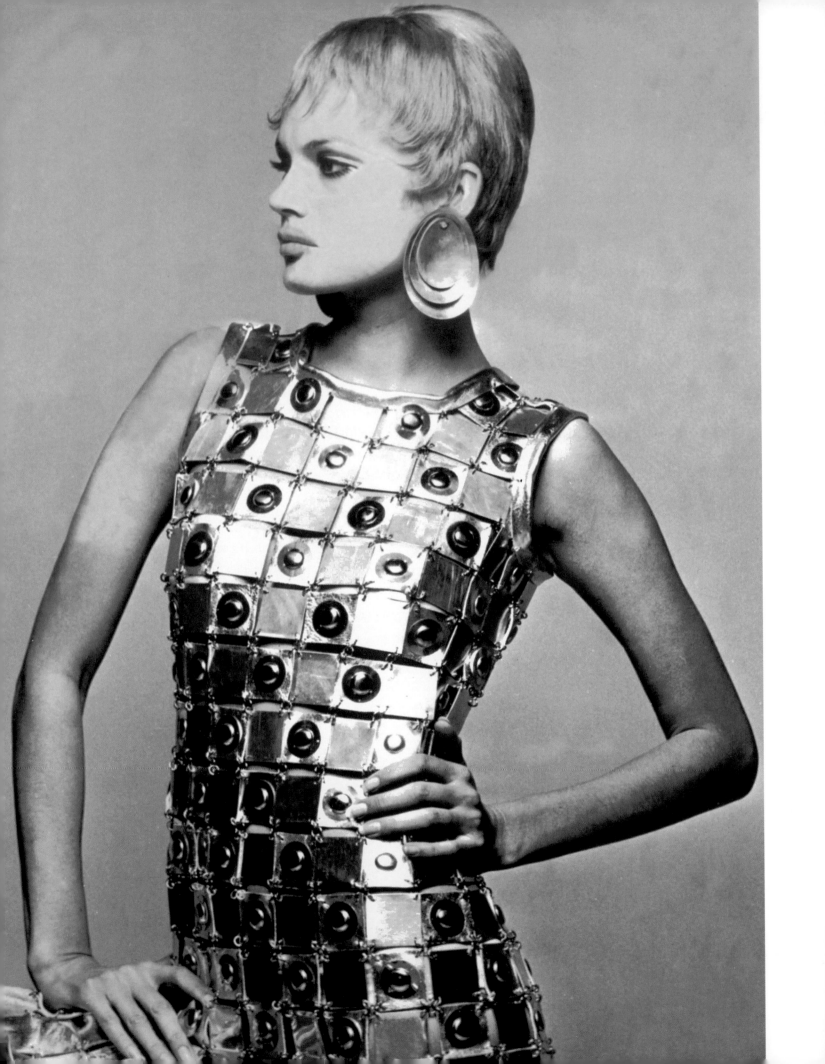

PACO RABANNE

chainmail minidress • 1966

Madman or genius? Artist or fashion designer? Paco Rabanne broke the boundaries between art, architecture, craft, and fashion, and helped to change a generation's attitude to clothing construction. Rabanne rejected the needle and thread for pliers and hammers. Instead of fabric, he chose small pieces of aluminum or plastic, stamped with holes and linked together with rings or rivets. The challenge was to create a flexible veil to flow over the body, but from rigid materials. Chanel snubbed Rabanne as a mere "metalworker." But the fashion establishment approved, and accepted him as a member of the Chambre Syndicale de la Couture in 1971.

Rabanne's chainmail minidresses became his trademark. This costume jewelry designer and son of a Balenciaga seamstress showed his first haute couture collection, "Twelve Unwearable Dresses," in Paris in 1966. Barefoot models wore dresses of linked plastic discs and plates. The fashion industry had never seen anything like it. *Vogue* claimed: "Suddenly everyone's talking about Paco Rabanne and his plastic fashion sculpture." By 1968 he was making dresses out of hammered and studded aluminum. Richard Avedon photographed model Penelope Tree wearing his shift dress of linked metal flowers. Bond girls wore Paco Rabanne, and the singer Françoise Hardy modeled his chainmail dress in real gold—it weighed nearly 20 pounds (9kg).

Rabanne encapsulated the spirit of the 1960s, a time of experimentation and obsession with the space age. His architectural training influenced his fascination with materials, particularly those traditionally used for interiors. Following in the footsteps of artist Marcel Duchamp, he raised mundane objects to high couture, with dresses of linked mother-of-pearl buttons and the metal plates used in butcher's aprons. He created new effects, using dried flowers or lace sealed between layers of plastic to make dresses. The press had a field day.

Comfort was not his priority. Women who chose to wear his metal dresses risked bruising themselves with the heavy, angular panels. Rabanne said in *Marie Claire* in 1967: "My clothes are weapons. When they are fastened they make the sound like the trigger of a revolver." Was it wise to wear metal so close to the skin? It could scorch the midriff in the sun of St. Tropez, and conduct the icy cold on an evening out in St. Moritz. But sometimes, nothing will stop a woman determined to make heads turn.

A Paco Rabanne dress made of metal squares held together by metal links, June 1967.

RAY-BAN SUNGLASSES

fashion classic • 1937

When the glare of the sun got too much for the Roman emperor Nero, it was said that he used an emerald to shield his eyes. Centuries later, experts confirmed that dark green helps absorb yellow light.

In the late 1920s, the U.S. Army Air Corps asked the Bausch & Lomb optical company to come up with antiglare lenses for the new breed of heroes in the sky as they darted and swooped under the sun, guns blazing. The new goggles with their special dark green lenses, free issue for pilots, did the trick. They were such a success that the entrepreneurs at Bausch & Lomb decided to sell the lenses to the public, but enclosed in an optical frame instead of goggles. Tinted glasses had been produced since the 1880s, but in civilian life had been a symbol of weak eyes. In 1937 Bausch & Lomb's aviator glasses came onto the market under the name Ray-Ban. They were the first sunglasses to be launched as a branded product.

Ray-Ban aviator sunglasses were exactly what 1930s Hollywood stars needed to protect them, not from the sun but from the glare of flashlights and publicity. The glasses veiled the eyes, hid emotion, and gave the stars a sense of privacy when they appeared in public. Flying was associated with the independent, modern woman. And thanks to the celebrity endorsement, sunglasses became cool.

Ray-Ban aviator sunglasses were exactly what 1930s Hollywood stars needed to protect them, not from the sun but from the glare of flashlights and publicity.

In 1952, Bausch & Lomb launched the Wayfarer Ray-Ban; Marilyn Monroe regularly wore a pair to deflect prying eyes. Ray-Bans hit the silver screen in movies such as *The Blues Brothers* (1980), lending extra star quality to Tom Cruise in *Top Gun* (1986), Clint Eastwood in *Dirty Harry* (1971), and Peter Fonda in *Easy Rider* (1969).

With the 1980s came a new wave of enthusiasm for the dark-lensed Wayfarer shades. In 1985 *The Face* magazine declared: "Black is the colour of the Eighties—anything already black, like Ray-Bans and rubber, is already in."

Ray-Bans complete the look for alien-hunters Tommy Lee Jones and Will Smith in Men in Black, *1997.*

ROLEX OYSTER WATCH

fashion classic • 1926

The Rolex crown logo says it all. The Rolex is top of the pile. King of the heap. Rolex can spit on the rest of the wristwatch world because it is internationally known as the best. Rolexes are the ultimate status symbols that stand for money, luxury, and quality. Each one is still entirely hand-made. They are passed down as heirlooms from father to son. And a Rolex watch is a street mugger's dream.

It all started with the Bavarian orphan Hans Wilsdorf. He opened a watch distribution firm in London in 1905, and cleverly began to promote the wristwatch as the timepiece of the future. He had the inner mechanism made in Switzerland. Wristwatches are for women, pooh-poohed his male critics, sticking to their large manly fob or pocket watches on chains. And anyway, they said, how can a watch on a moving wrist possibly keep accurate time?

When athlete Mercedes Gleitze swam the English Channel in 15 and a quarter hours in 1927, she wore a Rolex Oyster watch on her wrist.

A wristwatch, however, was the practical option for officers in the mud of the World War I trenches. They did keep time, and gradually they caught on. Wilsdorf strove for accuracy and precision, and he achieved it, proving the skeptics wrong. Kew Observatory in England awarded the Rolex wristwatch a class A precision certificate in 1914; up until then, this endorsement was bestowed only on marine chronometers. When athlete Mercedes Gleitze swam the English Channel in 15 and a quarter hours in 1927, she wore a Rolex Oyster watch on her wrist. Wilsdorf hailed it as the first airtight, waterproof, dustproof watch. The mechanism was sealed in a chamber, like Rolex Oyster watches today. In 1931 Rolex introduced one of the first self-winding mechanisms. In 1945 a window with a changing date was added to the face. And in 1953, for the intrepid only, came waterproofing for depths of 109 yards (100m).

Rolexes remain the royalty of the wristwatch world. And they've stood the test of time for almost a century.

A Rolex watch is one of the world's most instantly recognized—and widely imitated—symbols of efficiency and wealth.

JOHNNY ROTTEN

fashion icon • born 1956

It was June 1977. Britain was happily giving street parties and waving its little Union Jacks to commemorate 25 years of Elizabeth II's reign. The Silver Jubilee. Then along came punk band the Sex Pistols and kicked promonarchist Britain in the balls. Front man Johnny Rotten screamed and snarled the lyrics: "God save the Queen ... she ain't no human being.... There is no future ... In England's dreaming." The palace was not amused. But the public was. Despite a broadcasting ban, "God Save the Queen" rocketed to number two in the U.K. charts. Johnny Rotten (real name Johnny Lydon) and the Sex Pistols, spurred on by their manager Malcolm McLaren, had succeeded in rumbling the establishment.

Britain's youth could now infuriate its elders by wearing anarchy on its chests for just £3 ($5). The shops were awash with Jubilee mugs and coins, so the Sex Pistols launched their own souvenir. Their provocative God Save the Queen T-shirt showed a picture of the Queen with her

face pierced by a large safety pin. Those who dared wear one on London's streets at closing time in the summer of 1977 risked ending up in the gutter after a beery kicking. Graphic designer Jamie Reid, who came up with the image, suffered a broken nose and leg for wearing his own design.

Although T-shirts as standard rock memorabilia were already part of the U.S. music scene, Britain lagged behind. Malcolm McLaren pioneered using T-shirts to promote a band. "It's very important for kids to make statements, and that's exactly what a T-shirt does," a member of indie band Carter the Unstoppable Sex Machine, explained in *The Face* in 1991. By 1977 the printing presses were rolling off T-shirts in the U.K. Why shell out thousands of pounds to advertise when your fans could do it for you—and pay you for the privilege?

Dissatisfied youth loved the stream of subversive punk T-shirts produced by McLaren, his girlfriend Vivienne Westwood, and Reid. The shock-tactic T-shirt became an integral part of the punk movement. And Johnny Rotten became a punk hero.

Johnny Rotten, lead singer of the Sex Pistols, looks debonair in
tartan bondage, 1976.

YVES SAINT LAURENT

Le Smoking • 1966

In 1966 Paris fashion designer Yves Saint Laurent took up where Marlene Dietrich left off. He slipped a couple of sleek, satin-lapeled black pantsuits into his collection. Then, the following year, he made women's pantsuits the pivot of his show. His models swaggered down the runway in suits, white shirts, and dashing fedora hats. The press went wild.

Saint Laurent called the suit Le Smoking, the French word for a dinner jacket or tuxedo. The name stuck. His pantsuit reinterpreted men's evening dress for women. Worn with stilettos it could look flattering and feminine. The pantsuit set a trend as a sleek formal wear alternative for women, and they flew out of Saint Laurent's new ready-to-wear boutique, Rive Gauche. American *Vogue* editor Diana Vreeland was right when she wrote: "Follow Yves down the garden path. There's always a pot of gold at the end."

Le Smoking is one of Saint Laurent's most successful, and timeless, designs. Thanks to him, the women's trousersuit became respectable.

Women were ready for it—but the establishment was not. To them, a tailored suit still sent out signals which hinted at lesbianism and butch masculinity. But Saint Laurent challenged the idea that only a dress or skirt would do for formal occasions. Bianca Jagger wore a white pantsuit instead of a wedding dress when she married Mick. Lady Chichester, wife of yachts-man Francis Chichester, shocked by wearing a red pantsuit to her husband's knighthood in 1967. The pantsuit had become the height of daring chic.

The 1970s was the decade when women really began to wear the trousers, and androgyny flourished. Saint Laurent pioneered the look. "I finally got women into jersey, out of bras and into pants," he explained in *Vogue*, December 1969.

Le Smoking is one of Saint Laurent's most successful, and timeless, designs. Thanks to him, the women's pantsuit became respectable. And he still included a version of Le Smoking in his collections 30 years later.

Claudia Schiffer models a classic Le Smoking, autumn/winter 1996,
30 years after YSL launched his women's suits.

VIDAL SASSOON

five-point cut • 1964

London hairdresser Vidal Sassoon devised his geometric five-point haircut in 1964 on model Grace Coddington. Her picture appeared around the world. The sleek, helmet-style cut, with its long fringe, layered sides, and point at the nape of the neck, was something completely new. Fashion designer Mary Quant was photographed having her own five-point worked on by Sassoon, and it set a trend. Soon, all of young London wanted one too.

The simple, modern five-point epitomized 1960s youth fashion. Women dared to show their independence and defy their mothers by cutting off their hair. The short style meant liberation from weekly visits to the salon   a monthly trim was now enough. Sassoon broke with convention by letting the hair hang naturally flat, rather than forcing it into uncomfortable rollers. The five-point was low maintenance and designed to fall back into place at the shake of the head. For a night out on the tiles, modern girls could just slip on a minidress, brush, and go.

His new cut helped to raise Sassoon's profile from trendy hairdresser to style leader. The five-point is still Sassoon's most famous cut and, according to him, his most perfect. It was the ultimate geometric cut, with a severity inspired by architecture and the Bauhaus. Women loved the five-cut because it flattered the face, and emphasized the large painted eyes fashionable at the time. *Harper's Bazaar* lauded Sassoon in 1964: "His work possesses a new architectural clarity and, instead of muddying the planes of the face as some 'busier' bobs do, the Sassoon scissors throw them into striking relief." If a woman wasn't feeling brave enough to go for the chop, they could always get the look with a Sassoon wig instead.

> *The five-point is still Vidal Sassoon's most famous cut and, according to him, his most perfect. It was the ultimate geometric cut.*

The name "Vidal Sassoon" became synonymous with Swinging London. He collaborated with the major fashion designers of the day, including André Courrèges, Jean Muir, and Emanuel Ungaro. He cut the hair of starlets, models, and grandes dames. His salons were the place to be seen. And he still remains a household name today.

Vidal Sassoon's strikingly geometric cuts drew attention to the cat's eyes and thick lashes so popular in the 1960s.

ELSA SCHIAPARELLI
Circus collection • 1938

Elsa Schiaparelli kicked convention in the teeth with her outrageous and irreverent designs. The Schiaparelli style may have been shocking, but her clientele loved the eccentric Italian designer for her daring, offbeat, but beautifully executed clothes. The woman who invented "shocking pink" and made clothes with edible cinnamon buttons was also Coco Chanel's arch rival. Where Chanel produced soft, sporty, and practical clothes, Schiaparelli expressed herself with razor-sharp tailoring and wit.

Schiap (as she was known) is credited as one of the first designers to work a collection around a specific theme. Her Circus collection of 1938, inspired by the Barnum traveling circus, is a perfect example of the panache and originality with which the ex-student of philosophy approached fashion. Schiaparelli fused fashion and performance, drawing on the ideas of the dada and surrealist movements. It was a spectacle, and Paris was mesmerized. But Schiaparelli's playful attitude also shocked at a time when fascism was on the rise and the threat of war was becoming a reality.

In a chic Paris salon overlooking the Place Vendôme, her performers jumped on and off the desks in full circus costume. They ran up and down the stairs, walked the tight-rope, and juggled. They flew in and out of windows, with the help of ladders balanced precariously outside on the sidewalk. A ringmaster in a dapper high-collared jacket controlled the show. Schiaparelli, famed for her surrealist millinery, didn't disappoint with this collection. Her models wore hats based on an icecream cone, a chariot's wheel, inkpots and quills, and a brooding hen with buttons for eggs. They carried round bags designed to look like balloons and jackets with peppermint stick, licorice, and gingerbread buttons. Women pranced and paraded in daringly short tutus or wafts of torn chiffon. There were cufflinks in the shapes of roller-skates, show horses, ostriches, and bagpipes; buttons like swinging acrobats; boleros embroidered with performing elephants on stools and plumed ponies.

The Circus collection was Schiap at her very best, and it paved the way for the theatrical specta-cles that fashion shows would become by the end of the twentieth century.

Acrobat buttons and dancing horses on a Schiaparelli Circus jacket,
1938. Schiap was also noted for sleek, glamorous garments (above).

JEAN SHRIMPTON AND TWIGGY

fashion icons • 1960s

Jean Shrimpton, "the Shrimp," and Leslie Hornby, "Twiggy," were the two star models of 1960s Britain. Their skinny girl-child looks epitomized an era all-consumed with the pursuit of youth. They fueled public interest and became famous, paving the way for the supermodel phenomenon of the early 1990s.

A star was born when photographer of the decade David Bailey put convent girl Jean Shrimpton on the pages of *Vogue*. She shot to fame, and Bailey and Shrimpton became London's hottest couple for three and a half years. Bailey's lens gave the public tantalizing images of the Shrimp, with her innocent girl-next-door looks, shaking off formality and running free. Women wanted her blue doe eyes, natural gawky glamor, and long straight hair. "Bailey turned fashion pictures into portraits full of sexual imagery," explained Georgina Howell in her book *Sultans of Style*. "The stately drawing rooms were replaced by street markets and studio floors where Jean Shrimpton sprawled, skirts thigh-high, sometimes toying with a gun or cuddling a teddy bear."

"Twiggy is called Twiggy because she looks as though a strong gale would snap her in two and dash her to the ground.... The look of arrogance is a happy accident. Twiggy wouldn't know what arrogance means," declared *Vogue* in 1967. The 90-pound elfin waif with wide eyes, a crop by Leonard, and a fragile Lolita figure had the right looks to show off the pinafore dresses and miniskirts of the 1960s. With the backing of her hairdresser boyfriend Nigel John Davies, Twiggy became an international star.

Although *Vogue* condescendingly reported on her having "a lack of sophistication" and "a limited vocabulary," Twiggy was by no means stupid. She recognized that modeling couldn't last a lifetime. She capitalized on her name and negotiated licensing deals for Twiggy makeup, plastic dolls, clothing, and hosiery. She was named the Face of 1966, and then retired at a mere 19, but was coaxed back to star in the 1971 film *The Boyfriend*.

Left: Twiggy in a mini shirtdress, May 1967.
Right: Jean Shrimpton at Melbourne Races, November 1965.

WALLIS SIMPSON

fashion icon • 1896–1986

Wallis Simpson, who famously claimed that the fairer sex could never be too rich or too thin, married King Edward VIII in 1937. He sacrificed his throne for the twice-married American divorcée, and they became the Duke and Duchess of Windsor. The ceremony took place at the Château de Cande, near Tours in France. A room converted into a chapel. A chest doubled as an altar. It was the scandal of the decade.

All this couldn't have been better for Chicago-born fashion designer Main Rousseau Bocher, known as Mainbocher. He made Mrs. Simpson's trousseau and wedding dress, and as a result, became an international name. The public would never forget her Mainbocher blue-gray dress and matching jacket, and headpiece by Caroline Reboux. A sudden vogue for "Wallis blue" emerged. And the sleek wedding ensemble was copied and reproduced for the mass market. Romantics were seduced by the idea of giving up everything for love, and wanted a part of it.

"[Mainbocher] has given us not only the perfectly constructed dress, but also renewed our concepts of beauty and ease."

With the help of Mainbocher, reputedly her favorite designer, the Duchess of Windsor became an impeccably groomed style icon—never beautiful, but always chic. The duchess preferred the discreet covered-up look that Mainbocher did so well, rejecting some of the racier dresses of the 1930s. Mainbocher's signature style was classy and elegant, with streamlined dresses in bold colors cut on the bias to flatter the figure. "He has given us not only the perfectly constructed dress, but also renewed our concepts of beauty and ease," declared *Harper's Bazaar* in a 1967 retrospective of the designer's work.

By the time of Mrs. Simpson's marriage, Mainbocher had become the first American designer to open a couture house in France. His previous experience as fashion editor and then editor-in-chief of French *Vogue* made him an expert in dressing beautiful women. His very public work for the Duchess of Windsor catapulted him into the public eye—and it placed her on the world's best-dressed lists.

The Duke and Duchess of Windsor after their wedding in France, June 3, 1937.

Light, colorful, affordable, and accurate, Swatch watches introduced
a fun new approach to timekeeping.

SWATCH WATCH

fashion classic • 1983

The Swatch watch first hit the streets of the United States in 1983. Why were the watches with their bright straps and round plastic faces such a success? They were fun, sporty, durable, and irreverent. They summed up the sports fashion and bright colors of the 1980s, the decade when saying it loud was more important than subtle elegance. A Swatch advertisement in cult magazine *The Face* claimed: "All so wild, it'll make your head spin." And they were affordable, which meant that adults, teenagers, and children could all wear one. Swatch helped to change the notion of investing in one expensive watch for life—Swatches were Swiss-made, but at the same time cheap and cheerful fashion accessories that you could replace each year. Each watch was given a name, such as Black Magic, or Don't be too late.

But how did it all start? The Swatch was inspired by the world's thinnest gold watch, which, at less than an inch high (2.5cm), was developed in 1979. Its secret was its one-piece (rather than three-piece) case to hold the inner mechanical workings, and Swatch used the same principle to make its own slim design, but in plastic rather than gold. The new Swatch version was shock-proof, accurate, waterproof, and ideal for mass-production. They were constructed with just 51 components, rather than the traditional 90 or more pieces. Now, men and women never had to part with their efficient, battery-run timepiece that worked in the pool, on the slopes, and at the office. They could feel completely in control. By 1984 a million Swatch watches had been made, giving a much-needed a boost to the ailing Swiss watch market, which had been losing trade to East Asia.

> *Now, men and women never had to part with their efficient, battery-run timepiece that worked in the pool, on the slopes, and at the office.*

The plain Swatch face was like a blank canvas ready to be colored and decorated. The shapes stayed the same, but Swatch went to town with bright color and graphic design, calling in British fashion designer Vivienne Westwood and hip U.S. graffiti artist Keith Haring (described by Andy Warhol as "a man of the minute") to decorate the watch faces. The Swatch was a sign of the times and a fine example of 1980s design.

SWEATSHIRT

fashion classic • 1980s

By the end of the 1970s, exercise had become an obsession. *The Face* magazine wrote in 1988: "Those not following Fonda by going for the burn were out jogging or pumping iron—muscles became unisex." In 1982 Jane Fonda released her first workout video. And suddenly clothes previously relegated to the gym, the locker room, and the dance studio—rah-rah skirts, Calvin Klein's jock-strap underwear, leotards, legwarmers, and the sweat suit—were hot fashion items. Despite inducing heart attacks in middle-aged men, jogging (surely the most boring sport of all) became the fad and gray cotton jersey (sweatshirt material) the essential fabric.

The sweatshirt was a thick cotton sweater with a ribbed collar, hem, and cuffs, worn with its fleece lining next to the skin. Athletes had worn versions of them for warm-up exercises and practice since World War II. Women started to wear velour and toweling sweat suits as casual-wear during the 1970s, and in the following decade, sweats went designer.

Vivienne Westwood dressed her models in satin bras, worn over sweatshirts, for her Buffalo collection of the early 1980s. Designer Norma Kamali used the fleece-backed cotton of sweat suits in her 1981 Sweats collection—she added waists and shoulderpads to the sweatshirt, and teamed them with rah-rah skirts. By 1984 *Vogue* was promoting sweatshirt fabric, worn layered, draped, and tied.

The sweatshirt was the perfect canvas for the logos, slogans, and symbols that decorated clothing during the 1980s.

The Casuals (an early soccer-crazy youth group who wore branded sportswear), and the B-boys and flygirls (youth groups who dressed in the hip-hop style, influenced by New York breakdancers and rappers) of the 1980s, took tracksuits, sweatshirts, and sneakers off the track and onto the street. The Casuals wanted the expensive labels, while the B-boys and flygirls opted for anything obviously American. The sweatshirt was the perfect canvas for the logos, slogans, and symbols that decorated clothing during the 1980s. And it emulated the clothes of athletes and footballers, modern youth's role-models. These sportsman had everything to which kids aspired: status, respect—and money.

Originally designed as sportswear, during the 1980s the sweatshirt became popular as casualwear—for all ages.

TWINSET

fashion classic • 1950s

Ever the innovator, Chanel produced a twinset—a slip of a jersey cardigan worn over a matching jersey top—as early as 1918. The combination became popular as offduty casualwear in the 1930s, worn with sporty pants and skirts. But in the 1950s the twinset came to epitomize the height of luxury and chic—particularly if it was made out of expensive cashmere or angora.

The postwar "sweater girls," the curvy stars of the silver screen who pulled their tight knits over breasts coaxed into terrifying points, got the pulses racing of millions of teenage boys. In contrast, Grace Kelly, Jackie Kennedy, and Audrey Hepburn wore their "sweater sets" with their own idiosyncratic sense of classy, understated chic. In 1951 *Vogue* carried advertisements for the "All Wool Twin Set" in "moonstone, toffee, yellow, blush, and lavender," and promoted ice-blue twinsets for teenagers on its "Out of School" pages in the same year.

In the 1950s the twinset came to epitomize the height of luxury and chic—particularly if it was made out of expensive cashmere or angora.

Twinsets, and their accompanying pearls, became a symbols of British conservatism, along with the Aga stoves and tweeds of the Sloane Ranger. And no one fits this mold more than the queen. The *Guardian* reported on the Queen's visit to Milan in October 2000: "The monarch, whose four-day visit has seen her in a series of restrained pastel twinsets and pearls, brimless hats and diamond brooches, found the world's top designers falling over themselves to pay her homage: Gianfranco Ferre gushed about how much he admired the mixture of wool and cashmere in her slate grey two-piece and how well her black shiny handbag matched her black shiny shoes. Only Mariuccia Krizia injected a sober note. 'The Queen is above fashion. What she wears she wears well but she is not really a fashion lady.'"

But twinsets shed some of their frumpy image during the 1990s, when the demise of tailoring meant that fashionable women needed formal alternatives for the office and the evening. The twinset was the obvious answer. Now a cashmere Pringle twinset, for example, looked chic again, even with jeans. The sweater girls were back, this time without the pearls.

A twinset teamed with pearls, 1955. A classic during the 1950s, the twinset became fashionable again in the 1990s.

TYSON BECKFORD

fashion icon • born 1971

The beautiful muscle-bound Tyson Beckford was the face of Ralph Lauren's Polo Sport line, an offshoot of the American designer's Polo clothing label. Photographer Bruce Weber introduced Beckford to Lauren at a time when Tommy Hilfiger had championed the hip-hop fraternity with his street-cool designs. And, according to some, Tyson was exactly what Polo Sport needed. "Lauren's Polo Sport collection was foundering until 1995, when Lauren showed perfect hip-hop pitch when he signed the exotic African-American model Tyson Beckford as his poster boy under an exclusive contract that was reportedly valued at a million dollars a year—the brand's street credibility soared, putting it on a par with Tommy," wrote Teri Agins in her book, *The End of Fashion*.

Tyson grew up on the streets of Rochester, New York, and reputedly kept his head above water using the classic street survival tactics—drugs, guns, and gangs. He reputedly said that if he hadn't been discovered as a model, he would have either ended up dead or in jail. Instead, his tight six-pack, shaved head, and tattooed body made him a pin-up for the 1990s.

It was only when an editor from hip-hop magazine *The Source* spotted Tyson's good looks (he has Chinese and Jamaican ancestry, just like Naomi Campbell) that he had his chance to get out of the ghetto, via the catwalk. He signed up with a New York modeling agency, and went on to be named Model of the Year at the VH1 Fashion Awards, as well as one of *People* magazine's 50 Most Beautiful People.

Tyson is one of the few male models who has made supermodel status and who is known to consumers by name.

Tyson is one of the few male models who has made it to supermodel status and who is known to consumers by name. For a 1996 publicity coup for Lauren, he and fellow model Bridget Hall came roaring down the street, flanked by 50 Harley-Davidson riders, and stopped in front of Macy's store to sign autographs. His face has adorned covers of the best glossy magazines, and he will be remembered as the model who helped to make Ralph Lauren's Polo Sport cool.

A striking pose from Tyson Beckford, one of the best-known male models of all time.

EMANUEL UNGARO

trapeze-line coat • 1965

When Emanuel Ungaro opened his Paris couture house in 1965, he stunned the fashion establishment with his first collections. The bright oranges and pinks. The bold patterns. The hard geometric lines. Would anyone actually wear these screamingly loud prints that broke with convention? The answer was yes. Ungaro's clothes were new, freewheeling, and fun—and the youth market loved them.

The high-waisted, trapeze-line coats with interlocking geometric patterns became a trademark of these early collections. Ungaro's combination of razor-sharp tailoring and daringly loud fabric made a bold statement. He did not invent the narrow-shouldered, flared-hem trapeze line—Yves Saint Laurent had introduced that back in 1958. But Ungaro's interpretation of the trapeze line was so clean, so sharp that it looked new. The fabric fell from the angular shoulders in an unfalteringly straight line. He used very thick cloth, often fusing several layers together so that his coats held their shape.

Clean shapes that hung away from the body were a symbol of freedom and the future for disparate 1960s youth. Girls were longing to rebel against the curvaceous, all-woman silhouette of the 1950s, and Ungaro gave them the chance. He had already experimented with the clean, space-age aesthetic while working in the studio of the influential André Courrèges. Wild whispers whipped through the Paris ateliers that some of Courrèges's most successful 1960s designs were actually the inventions of Ungaro.

Cut and sew was in Ungaro's blood. He learned his trade from his tailor father. One of his first childhood toys was a sewing machine, and he made up clothes for his five-year-old sister. A spell at the House of Balenciaga taught Ungaro about proportion and color. And when he started his own collections, he collaborated with textile designer Sonja Knapp, who created some of his exuberant prints. One 1969 *Vogue* caption accompanying an Ungaro piece reads: "The painter's prints, luxurious, contemporary, just plain happy."

Ungaro may have experimented with line and color, but he always made sure that his clothes were wearable. His number one aim was to make women look their best.

A trapeze-style checked wool coat by Emanuel Ungaro, c.1965. The sculptured haircut is by Vidal Sassoon.

GIANNI VERSACE
printed silk shirt • 1980s

Bias-cut silk rippling over toned bodies. Pattern so opulent, so ostentatious that it teeters over the boundaries of good taste. Printed silk shirts were Italian designer Gianni Versace's trademark. They summed up everything that Versace stood for—luxury, glamor, sex. Silk on skin. Gold on a bronze tan. And they looked best on the supermodels who stormed the runways with their Barbie bodies and big hair. One classic photograph shows supermodels Christy Turlington, Linda Evangelista, and Helena Christensen, all in screamingly bright silk shirts, knotted at the waist and exploding with print—red, gold, printed jewels, putti, and ancient statues. As the *Independent on Sunday* put it in 1994: "The hallmark of his clothes, with their garish prints and triangular torsoed suits, is an overpowering sexuality which, without much imagination, turns men into studs and women into hookers."

Printed silk shirts found their way into most Versace collections during the 1980s and 1990s. Versace cut them on the bias so that they slipped seductively over the torso. He put silk with denim, leather, and lace, and, for inspiration, looked to the mistress of the bias cut, 1930s designer Madame Grès. Like Madame Grès's designs, Versace's shirts seemed effortless, nothing more than an extravagant silk square, secured onto the body with a few stitches. His secret was that he combined luxurious materials with simple, sporty shapes. Another obvious influence is his Italian predecessor Emilo Pucci, renowned for his printed resortwear of the 1950s and 1960s.

A fluid sheen of silk was the perfect fabric to show off his rich print designs. Versace exercised no restraint. Lisa Armstrong summed it up in the *Sunday Times*: "Versace has made vulgar and tarty an artform." His signature shirts veered from prowling yellow-and-black leopard prints to scrolls of gold on a black background. His colors were red, yellow, and purple. There were swirling paisleys, geometrically classical black-and-white patterns, and colored Warhol portraits. He translated Byzantine art, mosaics, and the gilt and iconography of Italy's Baroque churches onto his shirt fronts. And his signature emblem was the golden head of Medusa.

Fashion lost a unique talent when Gianni Versace was shot outside his Miami Beach mansion in 1997. The baton passed to his sister and muse, Donatella, to keep the Versace label alive.

Typically bold prints and screaming colors on the catwalk by the
master of ostentation, Gianni Versace.

The Duchess of Windsor packs in style: her Louis Vuitton luggage in the
back of her car, Paris, August 1952.

LOUIS VUITTON

trunk • 1854

Picture the scene. A trolley piled high with Louis Vuitton trunks and cases—the ultimate travel status symbol. It could be the docks by an ocean liner over 100 years ago. It could be Concorde's check-in today. The trunks carry with them a timeless whiff of elitism and luxury. When it comes to Louis Vuitton, you can tell a woman by her luggage.

The traditional travel trunk was dome-topped. But when trains and boats replaced carriages and stagecoaches, carpenter's son Louis Vuitton developed a flat-topped stackable trunk covered in gray varnished canvas. He cleverly made his cabin trunks to fit exactly under a ship's bunk. Vuitton trained as a trunk maker, so was familiar with the challenge of squeezing hooped crinolines and yards of silk into compact cases.

The wife of Emperor Napoleon III, Empress Eugénie, patronized Louis Vuitton. The great and the grand followed suit—Grand Duke Nicholas of Russia, Marlene Dietrich, Ernest Hemingway, the Duchess of Windsor. For renowned conductor Leopold Stokowski, Vuitton incorporated a writing desk with a foldout lid, so that he could work on his concert scores when traveling. For an Indian maharaja, he designed a traveling tea case complete with silver water carrier.

Of all Louis Vuitton luggage, it was the wardrobe trunk that ladies of fashion particularly prized. It was almost a home from home, with its hanging rails and small leather-handled drawers for precious clothes and fans.

New innovations came with the second generation of Vuittons. Louis's son, Georges, incorporated the five-tumbler lock, with its personalized number to ward off thieves. He also designed a waterproof, dustproof strap-on car trunk, much prized until car designers built in the trunk. And, thanks to Georges, the company introduced its trademark, the distinctive LV monogram. It was clever marketing—a monogrammed Vuitton trunk is instantly recognizable.

A further innovation came in 1959 with the third generation. Gaston-Louis Vuitton, son of Georges, devised a way of impregnating the canvas with a waterproofing formula. Now you could leave your trunks out in the rain for the passing world to admire.

VIVIENNE WESTWOOD

mini crini • 1985

When Vivienne Westwood's models teetered down the catwalk in platform shoes, tailored jackets, and swinging their little bell-shaped short hooped skirts, her 1985 Mini Crini collection became the laughing stock of Fashion Week. The "mini crini" itself was her short crinoline skirt, inspired by Victorian steel-hooped petticoats. No one had seen anything like this before. Her critics deemed them ridiculous, unwearable. But what they didn't know was that the collection would influence a new silhouette for the decade. .

Westwood's mini crini look is a prime example of her ability to sniff out a new trend, snatch at a feeling in the air, interpret it for the catwalk, and raise it to high fashion before her peers. She did it with punk, she did it with the New Romantics, and now she was doing it with the short bell-shaped skirt. Other designers soon picked up on the trend. When Christian Lacroix took the revolutionary step of opening a couture house in 1987, his signature pieces became his short, puffed-up balloon skirts. The puffball skirt, with its hems that looped under and stitched to the lining, became a hit on the high street.

Westwood's mini crini is a prime example of her ability to sniff out a new trend ... interpret it for the catwalk, and raise it to high fashion before her peers.

"I don't really care about the press. I used to be upset by it, but now it doesn't upset me," explained Westwood in a 2001 interview in the *Guardian* newspaper. "It's just annoying when you do what in my opinion is the best show of the whole season and there are no pictures of it, and in a few years someone else will copy it and everyone will think it's new."

Born in Derbyshire, England, the princess of punk, who had no formal fashion training, broke the taboos of a century by airing the secrets of the bedroom in public. For punk, in the 1970s, she promoted fetish and bondage garments. In the 1980s, she raised underwear to outerwear with her infamous corset tops and mini crinis. And when she went to Buckingham Palace in 1992 to receive her OBE from the Queen, she innocently swirled up her skirts for the cameras. Had she really forgotten that she had got no underpants on? Well, what do you think...?

British model Iris Palmer trips along the catwalk in a Toile de Jouy-print Westwood mini crini.

*Walking tall: vertiginous Westwood lace-up platform soles and
high heels tower above the competition.*

VIVIENNE WESTWOOD

platforms and heels • 1984

Grande dame of punk. Genius. English eccentric. However you describe Vivienne Westwood, the flamboyant British designer who rides her bicycle in her trademark platform shoes, there is no denying her conviction. And the platform shoe was one idea she just wouldn't give up on.

In 1984 the world thought that platform soles had been buried along with the faded glitter of 1970s glam rock. But Westwood dug them up, and put six-inch (15cm) platforms designed by Patrick Cox on the catwalk. To accompany her 1987 Harris Tweed collection, Westwood introduced her famous rocking horse platforms, complete with upturned wooden soles resembling a pair of clogs. Some had ballerina leather straps winding around the ankles, while the "golf" version had a tassel. Soon every fashionista was clattering along London's pavements, looking like a cross between a ballet dancer and something out of a Carl Larsson painting. Rocking horse shoes are still in demand, 15 years after their inception.

In 1990 Westwood took her platforms one step further. She asked John Amathus, who handmade her shoes in his Bow Street factory, for a hidden platform shoe. He incorporated the sole into the shoe itself, and used one continuous piece of leather to cover both the side of the shoe and the sole. The effect was like a large, shiny, leather clubfoot. You couldn't miss it.

By 1993 Westwood's shoes challenged the fashion elite to live even more dangerously, with "super elevated" platforms boasting heels over 10 inches (25cm) high. "Standing among these models, I am struck by how tall they are. At over six feet and in platform shoes they tower like a race of giants," wrote Fred Vermorel about a Westwood show in his book, *Vivienne Westwood: Fashion, Perversity and the Sixties Laid Bare.* And it was due to a super-elevated pair in blue mock-croc that catwalk veteran Naomi Campbell took a public tumble on the Paris runway.

Thanks to Westwood's perseverance, platform shoes were back in mainstream fashion by the early 1990s. But some of her own designs are anything but mainstream. They are museum pieces, designed for the catwalk (Campbell's blue ones are displayed in London's Victoria & Albert Museum). These theatrical pieces are hard to resist—black-patent leather with fins of metal studs; red, white, and blue lace-up platforms like the French flag, and even platforms with a gold-plated heel. Shoe fetishists eat your hearts out.

'YOU HAVE TO DESTROY TO CREATE' MALCOLM McLAREN

'THE ABILITY TO LAUGH AT THE THIEVES' SITUATION 3

VIVIENNE WESTWOOD PHOTOGRAPH BY NORMA MORICEAU

VIVIENNE WESTWOOD

clothes for Seditionaries • 1976

Darlings of the avant-garde and precursors of punk, Vivienne Westwood and Malcolm McLaren renamed their King's Road boutique Seditionaries in 1976. The shop exterior was ambiguous—sheets of white opal glass, neon tubes, and a brass plaque bearing the words: "Seditionaries. Malcolm McLaren and Vivienne Westwood. Clothes for Heroes." Inside, ceiling-to-floor photographs of Dresden after its shameful bombing by the British in World War II and a special table holding a live rat greeted those brave enough to make it past the front door. This was where the early punks came to get their clothes.

The Seditionaries clothes of 1976 to 1979 appealed to the youth of the late 1970s, and shocked the older generation. Fred Vermorel, in his book on Westwood, explained: "We were selling clothes for a commitment to anarchy and people were walking around on the streets in clothes you only saw before in the bedroom." McLaren's protégés, outrageous punk band the Sex Pistols, made the perfect models.

While the self-taught Westwood designed most of the clothes, McLaren provided provocative slogans and graphics for the Seditionaries T-shirts. One read, "For soldiers, prostitutes, dykes and punks." The word "Destroy," an inverted crucifix, a swastika, and lyrics from the Sex Pistols' song "Anarchy in the U.K." all appeared on one muslin shirt.

Westwood painted and bleached stripes onto shirts. She sold bondage pants and parachute shirts wound and wrapped with straps. Her earrings featured male genitalia in miniature. She made some clothes from scratch, while others were customized, but she always insisted on using good-quality fabrics—hence the high price tags of Seditionaries clothes. The clothes were not pretty, but neither was punk. And they took guts to wear.

As punk violence began hitting the newsstands, Seditionaries fashion started to trickle onto the newspapers' fashion pages. But by 1979 the Sex Pistols' Sid Vicious was dead of a heroin overdose, and punk was becoming increasingly drug-addled. McLaren and Westwood sensed it was time for a change. In 1980 they renamed the shop World's End, and Westwood began thinking of pirates and the French Revolution. She was about to launch the New Romantic look.

Vivienne Westwood wears one of her own designs for Seditionaries:
punky, provocative, and intended to shock.

Index